M5 / M5A1 Stuart

Written by Jim Mesko

Walk Around®

Cover Art by Don Greer

Line Illustrations by Matheu Spraggins

Squadron/Signal Publications

(Front Cover) ***MICKEY GEORGIANA,*** **an M5A1, serves with the 4th Armored Division in Sartilly, France, in July 1944.**

(Title Page) This beautifully restored M5A1 was part of the collection at the now defunct World War Two Learning Center in Youngstown, Ohio. The tank is now part of a collection in Florida.

(Back Cover) ***EL ALAMEIN,*** **an M5A1, serves with the 2e Demi-Brigade of the French Expeditionary Force in Indochina in 1946.**

About the Walk Around®/On Deck Series®

The Walk Around®/On Deck® series is about the details of specific military equipment using color and black-and-white archival photographs and photographs of in-service, preserved, and restored equipment. *Walk Around®* titles are devoted to aircraft and military vehicles, while *On Deck®* titles are devoted to warships. They are picture books of 80 pages, focusing on operational equipment, not one-off or experimental subjects.

Proudly printed in the U.S.A.

1115 Crowley Drive, Carrollton, TX 75006-1312 U.S.A.

ISBN 978-0-89747-610-2

Military/Combat Photographs and Snapshots

If you have any photos of aircraft, armor, soldiers, or ships of any nation, particularly wartime snapshots, please share them with us and help make Squadron/Signal's books all the more interesting and complete in the future. Any photograph sent to us will be copied and returned. Electronic images are preferred. The donor will be fully credited for any photos used. Please send them to:

Squadron/Signal Publications
1115 Crowley Drive
Carrollton, TX 75006-1312 U.S.A.
www.SquadronSignalPublications.com

Dedication

This book is dedicated to armor collectors Henry Venetta and Jacques Littlefield, and armor enthusiasts Art Gerber, Ray Gill, Chris Saulet, and Yves Christen. God bless you and may you rest in peace, my friends.

Acknowledgments

Special thanks to Lance Miller for allowing me access to his restored M5A1 and to Kevin and Jim Hess for introducing me to him. Bill Klingbeil, Duane Ward, Gary Binder, Rob Ervin, Bob Steinbrunn and Mike Green provided photos. Dick Hunnicutt, The Patton Armor Museum (PAM), The World War Two Learning Center, Steve Zaloga, and Kurt Laughlin provided support through photos or published information. All photos are credited to their sources. Uncredited photos were taken by the author.

Introduction

The M5 and M5A1 series represent the culmination of the development of the M3 "Stuart" tank. This final "Stuart" version took shape as the U.S. Army realized that surging demand for aircraft would cut into the supplies of engines available for tank production.

The Cadillac Division of General Motors suggested that the M3 be modified to take twin Cadillac automobile engines connected to a Hydramatic automatic transmission in mid-1941. Under the designation M3A2 this configuration was tested and found acceptable. The Army therefore approved production of the vehicle, eliminating the need for the Continental radial engine that had powered the M3 series.

The new light tank's initial designation of M4 was soon changed to M5, in order to avoid confusion with the M4 "Sherman" tank then in production. In addition to the new power plant, the M5 also featured a redesigned welded hull with a sloped front glacis plate that provided better ballistic protection, although the side armor was still vertical. The new design provided more interior room for the crew.

The forward hatches of the M3 were replaced on the M5 with overhead hatches for the driver and assistant driver. Each had a rotating M6 periscope for indirect observation, and a two-inch hole for direct vision that could be covered by mushroom-shaped steel plugs.

The rear of the hull was "stepped up" to accommodate the new Cadillac engines and radiators. Elimination of the early M3's prominent external air filters gave the new tank a much smoother appearance.

The M5 incorporated the relatively small M3A1 turret that featured "pistol ports" on both sides and mounted the same 37mm cannon as carried on the M3, with a co-axial .30 caliber machine gun. Also mounted on the hull was a .30 caliber machine gun for the assistant driver's use. Two triangular hatches, flush with the top of the turret, were provided for the commander and gunner, and a radio was mounted in the hull.

The Cadillac Motor Car Division and the Massey Harris Company began producing the new vehicle in the spring of 1942.

While the M5 was under development, the Army was also working on the M3A3, the final version of the M3 series. The M3A3 resembled the M5 with its sloped hull, but its turret and sloping side armor were new. In line with a British idea, a bustle housing a radio was built into the M3A3 turret, which had bigger commander and gunner hatches.

The turret initially also featured pistol ports on both sides, but these were later eliminated as being of little use and because they compromised armor integrity. An external mount for a .30 caliber machine gun was then relocated from the turret's rear to its right side, replacing one pistol port. The ports, initially plated over, were totally eliminated as production geared up. The new turret was later added to the M5, which was then designated the M5A1.

The new models incorporated the M3 series vertical volute suspension, with four mounts and two bogie wheels in each unit. Initially both the bogie wheels and the rear idler wheel had open spokes. Later the openings were plated over. Then the Kelsey-Hayes Wheel Company developed a stamped bogie wheel that began to appear on vehicles in 1943, though some spoked-wheel M5s were still around at the end of the war.

A rare M5 is on display at the 1st Infantry Museum in Cantigny Park, Wheaton, Illinois. There is an early pistol port between the grousers on the side of the turret.

This early-production M5A1 at Camp Borden, Ontario, Canada, shows the lengthened turret bustle on this turret adapted from the M3A3 series. The bustle housed the radio after it was moved from inside the hull.

The primary difference between the M5 and the M5A1 is the turret. The M5 used the basic turret from the M3A1, which was smaller and rounded in the rear. The commander and gunner each had his own triangular-shaped hatch. (Patton Armor Museum [PAM])

The M5A1 uses the M3A3 turret, which features a bustle at the rear to house a radio. In addition, the hatches for both the commander and gunner on the M5A1 were substantially enlarged. (PAM)

The pistol ports were eliminated fairly early in the M5A1 production run. This M5A1 at the Patton Museum also features the later stamped road wheels that eliminated the threat of having a steel bar jammed into the spoked version, which would stop the tank.

The late-production M5A1 features an armored mount into which the .30 caliber machine gun could fold for protection when not in use. The new armored shield for the machine gun altered the previous clean symmetrical lines of the M5 turret.

The most recognizable difference between the M3 and M5 is the smooth, front-sloped glacis plate of the new M5 version. This sloped front eliminates numerous shot traps. The driver and assistant driver hatches were relocated to the top of the hull.

The M5 series is much more streamlined than the early M3 series. The welded hull was extended forward. The use of a new drive train allowed more interior room.

The use of the twin Cadillac engines and their radiators resulted in the M5's rear hull being raised to accommodate the engine mountings. The new hull eliminated the externally mounted air filters of the early M3.

Access to the engines is through two sets of doors at the rear. Exhaust deflectors were added above and below the doors, starting with the intermediate production run. This vehicle displays a later-production-run modification that allowed the addition of a towing pintle. (Rob Ervin)

A deep-fording kit has been installed on this M5, whose various hull and turret openings have also been sealed up. The anticipated use of tanks in amphibious operations led to the development of deep-fording equipment. (PAM)

An M5 undergoes amphibious tests. The sealed cooling intake and exhaust stack limited the time the vehicle could operate in this condition before the engine quit. (PAM)

This M5A1 features another style of fording equipment. The pistol ports have been welded over on this early vehicle. (PAM)

Wading gear completely encloses the rear of the lower hull, necessitating the removal of the exhaust deflectors. The lines running back from the turret allowed the gear to be jettisoned immediately after landing. (PAM)

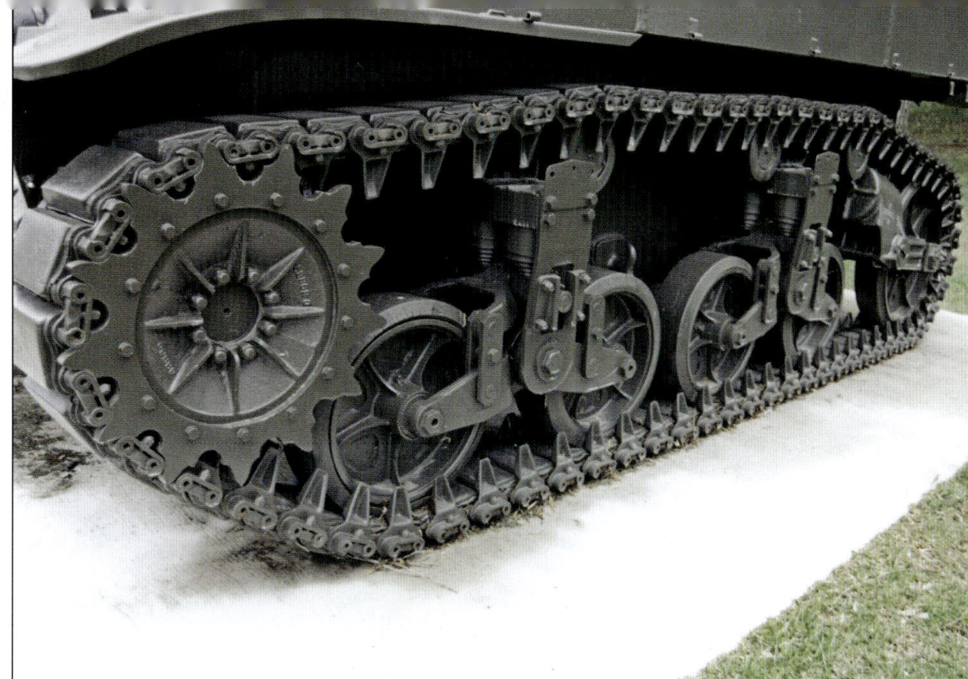

The M5 series used the M3 series' vertical volute suspension that featured a front-mounted drive sprocket, two sets of bogie wheels, and a rear mounted idler wheel that was adjustable for track tension.

Fairly early in production a new sprocket with 13 teeth replaced the older one. The final drive ratio was changed to 2.57:1. This new drive sprocket was about two inches smaller in diameter than the 14-tooth sprocket.

The initial drive sprocket on the M3 series has 14 teeth and a 2.4:1 final drive ratio. The sprocket rings are bolted onto the main hub and can be replaced.

The inner and outer sprockets are identical and interchangeable. The interchangeability of tank components made for ease of replacement and simplified the supply system. Interchangeability also gave the U.S. forces a tremendous advantage over the Germans in keeping the maximum number of tanks in service.

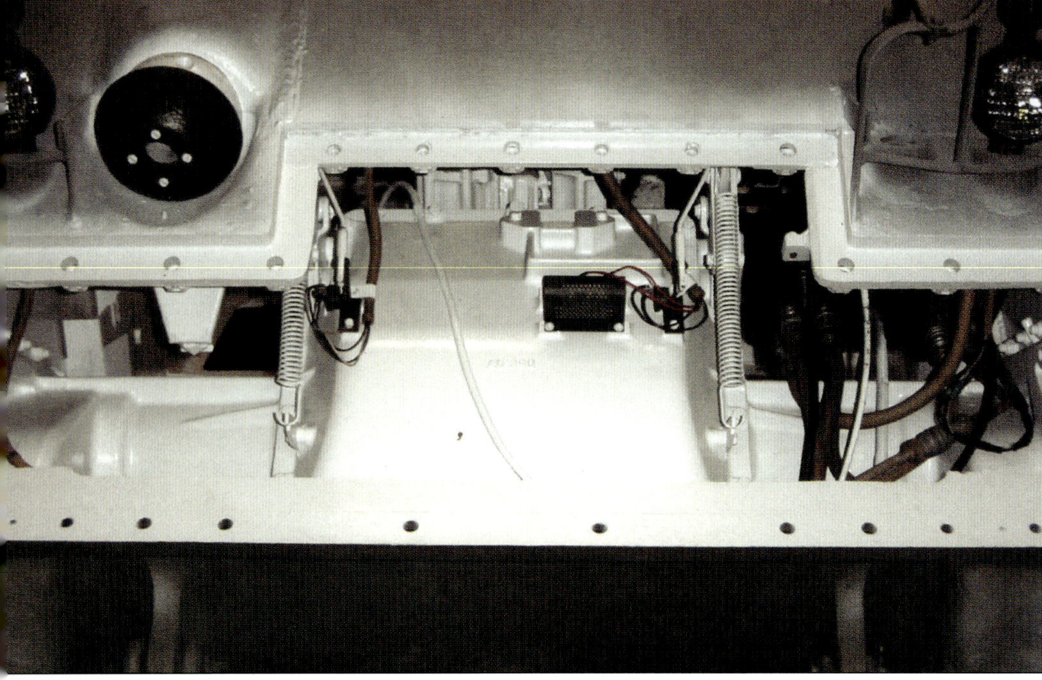

The relatively easy unbolting and removal of the lower hull plate exposes the heart of the final drive, which is located in front of the two drivers, with the transfer case dividing the compartment. (Lance Miller)

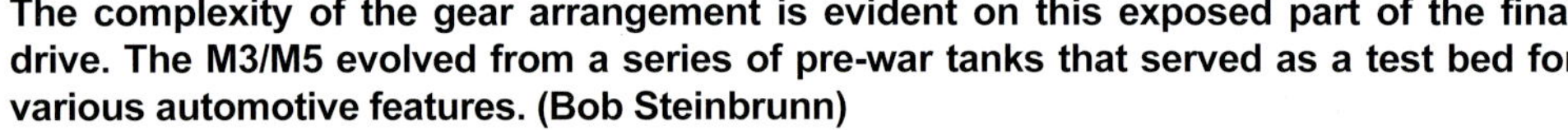

The complexity of the gear arrangement is evident on this exposed part of the final drive. The M3/M5 evolved from a series of pre-war tanks that served as a test bed for various automotive features. (Bob Steinbrunn)

With the transfer casing removed, the connecting points between the transfer case and final drive become visible. The M5 series was noted for its reliability and relative ease of maintenance. (Bob Steinbrunn)

The inside of the transmission housing is seen here exposed after its cover has been unbolted and removed. The sprocket attached to the power train coming through the hole on the hull wall. (Bob Steinbrunn)

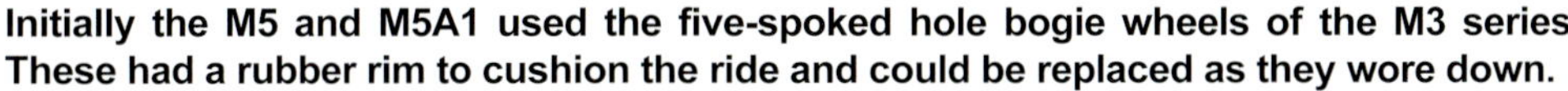

Initially the M5 and M5A1 used the five-spoked hole bogie wheels of the M3 series. These had a rubber rim to cushion the ride and could be replaced as they wore down.

The Kelsey-Hayes Wheel Company came up with a stamped metal wheel cover to replace the old spoked version. Production began in 1943 under the designation C107928. The nipples for greasing the hub are in the indentations on the bogies. The added plate on the face of the suspension is for attaching sand shields.

To make use of the spoked wheels already on hand, the holes were plated over to prevent anything being jammed in them to stop the tank. This was based on experience in battle against stubborn Japanese resistance in the Pacific.

The rubber on the rims can wear down and even break off. The pop rivets around the inner rim help hold the outer rim in place. While the Germans suffered from a rubber shortage, the American war industry never experienced such a lack of material.

The outer metal rim had groves and a raised outer edge to help hold the rubber rim firmly in place.

The suspension assemblies are attached to axles that span the entire width of the hull. The axles were fit into U-shaped troughs that are bolted on to the bottom of the vehicle.

The suspension consists of hinged front and rear arms connected to a spider link arm. Atop the arm are two sets of volute springs attached to a bracket. On top of the bracket is a skid.

The suspension arms were attached to each axle end. Each arm operated independently of the other, thereby giving the suspension good movement over rough terrain.

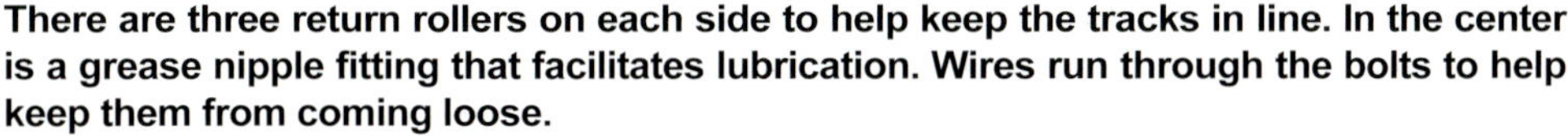

There are three return rollers on each side to help keep the tracks in line. In the center is a grease nipple fitting that facilitates lubrication. Wires run through the bolts to help keep them from coming loose.

At the rear of the vehicle is the idler wheel. The idler arm holding the wheel was attached to a bracket that contained a volute spring. The original idler wheel was the steel-rimmed D34910 that was used on the M3.

Hooks are welded between the bogie housing on each side of the vehicle. The hooks were used for attaching cables and chains, or to help tie down the tank. The numerous weld beads around the fitting greatly strengthened the joint and allowed tremendous pressure to be placed on the hook.

The later-style rubber tired idler wheel has smaller teardrop-shaped holes than those on the D34910. This wheel was designated the C107939.

Turning the bolt on this arm tightens or loosens the tension on the idler wheel.

To cover the holes between spokes, plates were welded on one side of wheel. Normally, the practice was to place the welded side on the inside of the wheel. The ability of American industry to update and utilize older components helped maximize equipment supply throughout the war.

Since the open-spoked idler, like the spoked bogie wheel, was susceptible to being jammed, plates were welded between the idler spokes, as was done with the bogies.

Another idler wheel pattern had very small holes, and the inner faces of these too were plated over. There was also a wheel that had no openings at all. These patterns were rarer than the teardrop shapes.

The bracket holding the idler arm and volute spring is bolted onto the side of the hull. Lubrication points for both the idler arm and wheel are marked in red. A skid is mounted on top of some brackets.

A volute spring is located inside the bracket. The flange extending upward from the idler arm would compress this spring as the tank moved up a slope. This limited how much of a slope the tank could climb.

The most common track used was the T16E1, which was a rubber-blocked, double-pinned, 11.6-inch-wide track with reversible pads. It also came in a non-reversible version, the T16E2.

The track pads wear down until they reach a point like this where they need to be reversed. How fast they wear down depends on the type of terrain over which they travel.

While the pads on the outside wear down, the sides facing inward suffer little, if any, significant wear. When the pads reach a certain point they can be reversed, giving the tank a whole new tread surface.

Besides the T16 rubber-padded track, the M5 was sometimes fitted with the T36E6 steel parallel grouser track. It could also run on the T55E1 steel chevron track. The widely used rubber pad tracks were more common, however.

The glacis plate is bolted down to the lower hull with combinations of oval or hex-head screws, depending on the manufacturer. An oil access hole was situated under the top two bolts on the final drive housing.

The overlap of the lower glacis plate hides the nuts into which the bolts are screwed. Ten screws hold the horizontal plate in place.

Underneath the final drive cover a series of bolts attach the cover to the lower hull.

Most of the M5 series structure consists of rolled steel plate, held in place by extensive welding. The irregular weld lines show that all welding was done by hand.

Screws hold the engine deck in place. On early models, these screws and the entire upper deck had to be removed to access the radiator and engines. Later models featured four sections that facilitated easier access to the engine.

The rear hull is composed of four steel plates welded together. The various fittings were then either bolted or welded down on the assembly.

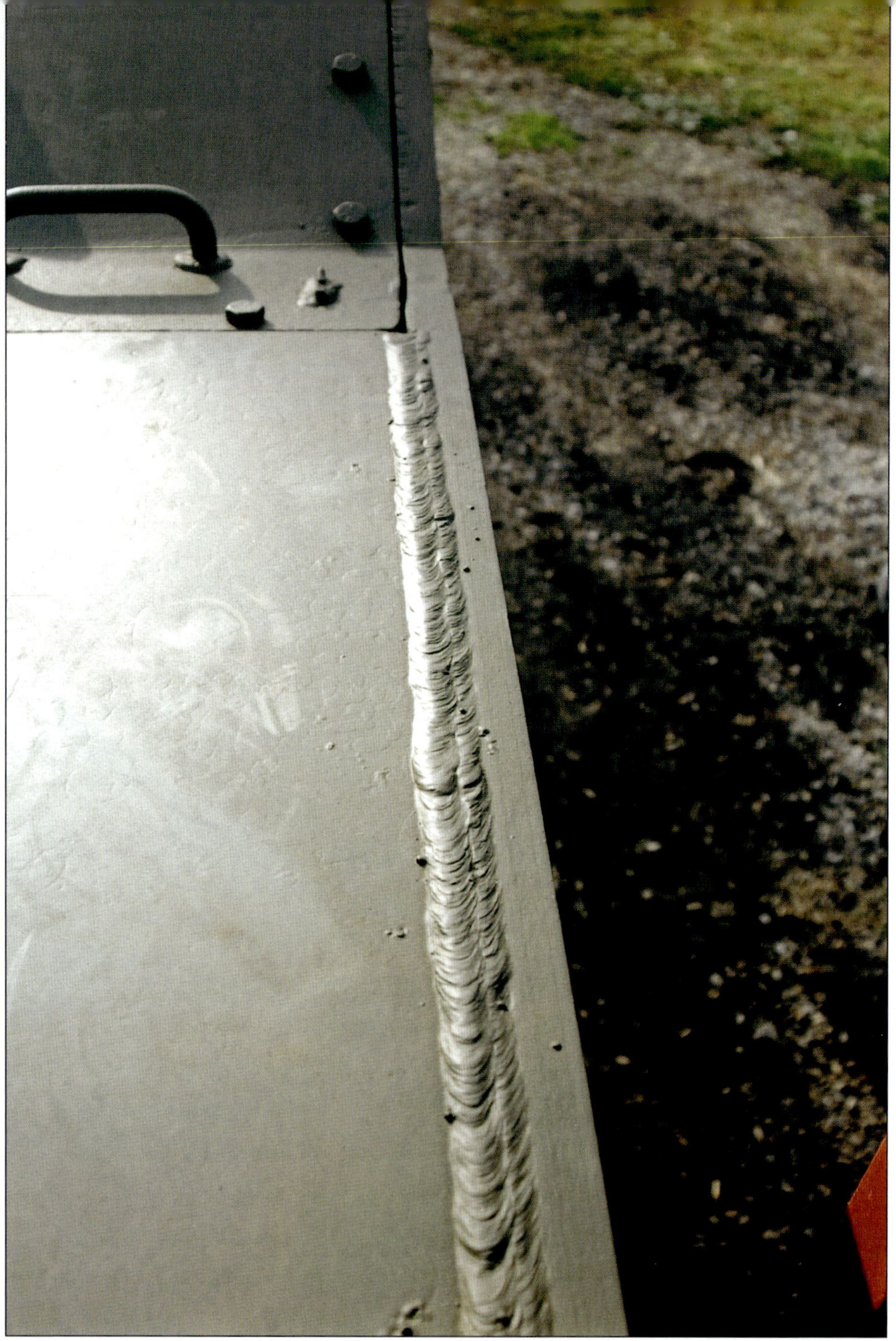

The upper hull is welded to the side armor plate all the way back to the engine deck.

The entire upper hull is welded to the sponson section that, in turn, is welded to the lower hull. The cast cap is the drain plug for the fuel tank.

The cast cap is held in place by four nuts. This view shows the drain plug with the cap removed. One of the screws for the bolts has broken off.

The front fenders project to a point about even with the front of the tank. Made of sheet metal, the fenders were easily dented or ripped off during combat operations. (Rob Ervin)

When sandshields, here seen bolted onto the fenders, were introduced in early 1943, the sprocket covers had embossed ribs on their sides for additional strength. (Rob Ervin)

The sprocket covers also cover the inner portion and are bolted onto the fender attachment point on the hull. (Rob Ervin)

The sand shield panel over the bogie assemblies hangs from hinges on the fenders. The sandshields were also bolted to supports on the bogies.

To support the sandshields, extensions were added to the bogie brackets. The shields were supported by a single flange bolted on the extension and on bottom of the shield.

A small door providing access to the air cleaners was located in the rear sandshield cover over the idler. The covers helped to keep down dust, but provided absolutely no protection against enemy fire, and were easily torn off.

The sandshields wrap around the rear fenders and come into contact with the lower rear of the hull. Their flimsy construction meant that they were very easily damaged or ripped off in the field.

In front of the driver's position are a headlight and siren. The brush guard design was originally symmetrical but later was raised above the headlight.

Another headlight is mounted in front of the assistant driver next to the hull .30 caliber machine gun position. Four screws hold the machine gun's cast ball mount in place.

The machine gun, attached from the inside, is intended for general suppression fire. When moving, accurate fire was impossible for the assistant driver, due to the constant motion of the tank. (Bill Klingbeil)

The arc of fire is limited to the right by the fender and brush guard. There is a greater arc to the left. The hole above the machine gun is the direct vision port that can be covered by a mushroom shaped plug attached to a chain, not fitted here.

The brush guards are welded onto the hull and have supporting arms for additional support. Where the arms attach to the main guard can vary. The lightweight guards are surprisingly strong.

Later-production M5A1s have provisions for a driver's windscreen. Visible here are the brackets for holding the windscreen in place when not in use.

The rectangular object at the bottom of the windscreen, seen here in the stowed position, is the windshield wiper mechanism. The wiper is above the mechanism. (Duane Ward)

The windscreen is in the upright position with the driver's canvas hood in place. Cumbersome to hook up, the hood could not prevent water from seeping in, particularly in view of the downward slant of the hull. (Bill Klingbeil)

This ring attached to the frame on the front of the hull holds the screen in the upright position. Pulling the lever down loosened the ring, allowing the windscreen to be folded down or removed. Although the windscreen was held tightly in place by the ring, it could not prevent water leaks. (Bill Klingbeil)

The canvas hood, seen here from behind, completely covers the driver's open hatch. Though not water-tight, the hood offers some protection from the elements. But since it prevents the hatch from closing, the hood was only used on road marches when combat was not expected. (Bill Klingbeil)

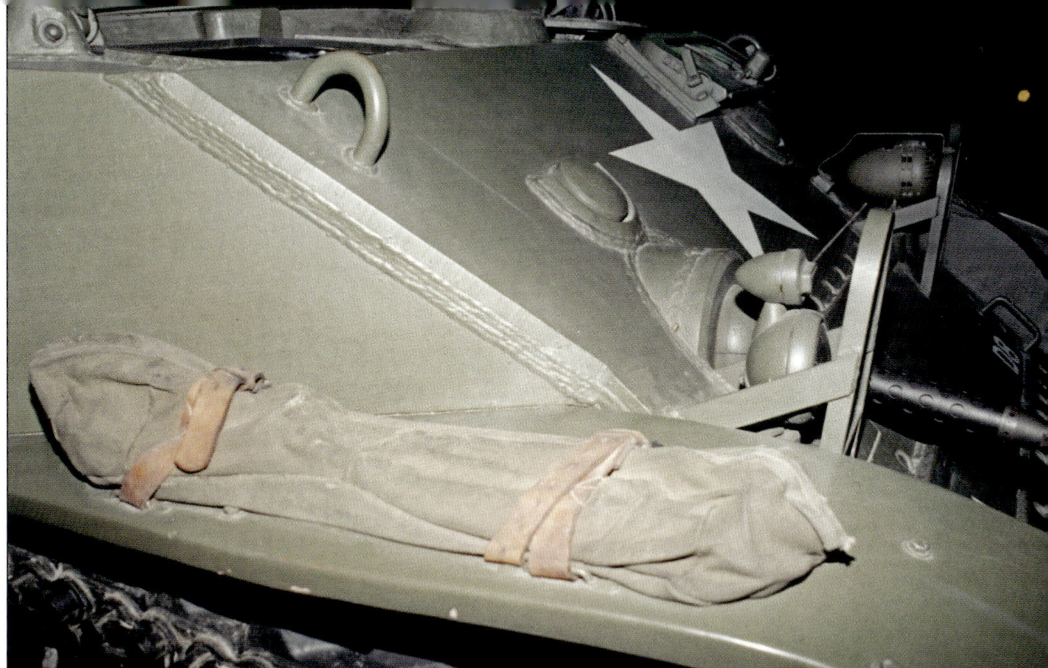

The small brackets welded to the fender are tie downs for equipment. They are found on both fenders.

As seen in this museum example, gear can be wrapped in canvas and held down on the fender by leather straps. Although it obviously varied from crew to crew, gear was sometimes stowed in the field in this manner.

Later-production vehicles feature a holder for a shovel on the forward portion of the fender. The flimsy fenders could be easily ripped off if the tank ran into some substantial object. Crews were careful with additional gear they stored on the fender tie downs.

Leather straps hold the shovel. Two straps are used for the front of the shovel. Wooden handles could be either olive drab, black, or left in natural wood finish.

The driver and assistant driver each had his own hatch through which to enter or leave his position. The hatches were mirror images of each other.

The hatches pivot on mounts at the rear outer corner of each hatch. A grease nipple can be seen on the end of the welded-on mount.

Both hatches open outward from the center line of the hull.

When upright, the hatch inclines slightly past 90° vertical toward the back. A simple mechanism allows it to be locked open to prevent its falling back onto the driver's head. The locking pin at the top is engaged when the hatch is in the closed position.

Each hatch features an indirect-vision M6 periscope that rotates 360°. These retractable periscopes are protected by a brush guard and covered by a spring-operated top. (Bill Klingbeil)

Vision through the periscope is limited. Crews preferred open hatches if conditions permitted. Although the periscopes could rotate 360°, the actual field of vision is much more limited, due to the drivers' small work area and the turret directly behind them.

When the hatch is closed, the M6 periscope is positioned at approximately the driver's height when seated. The height of the seats is adjustable by using a spring-operated mechanism. The hatch interiors are painted the same as the exterior of the vehicle in order not to stand out when opened.

Between the drivers' hatches is an oval-shaped ventilation hatch, a feature not found on early-model vehicles. There is a small hole in the front to allow water to drain out.

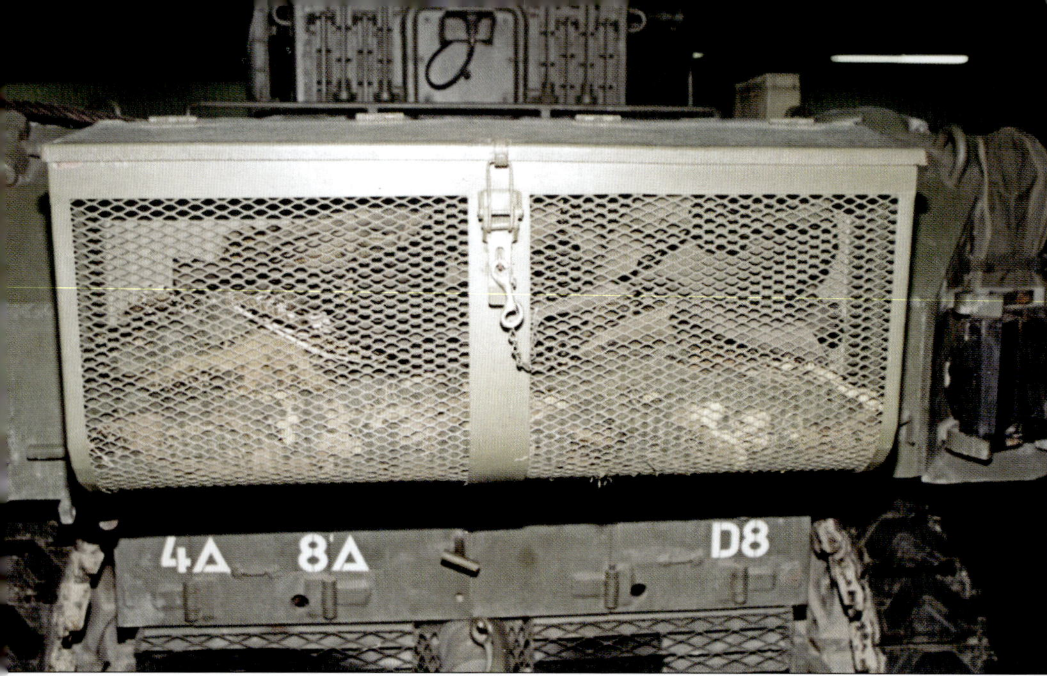

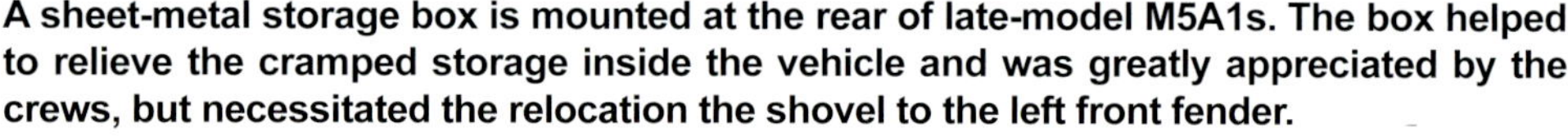

A sheet-metal storage box is mounted at the rear of late-model M5A1s. The box helped to relieve the cramped storage inside the vehicle and was greatly appreciated by the crews, but necessitated the relocation the shovel to the left front fender.

A bracket secures the stowage box to the hull. The “L”-shaped flange welded to the box is bolted to a fitting welded on the hull. (Rob Ervin)

The storage box runs down the rear slope of the hull and against the vertical rear panel. It is secured to the hull by several brackets, one of which can be seen at the bottom.

The box, located between the rear lights, features several tie-down attachments and clasps to secure it during road movement. The sheet metal provides no protection against enemy fire and makes access to the engine compartment a little more difficult.

The wire mesh cage of the storage box allows for drainage and air flow to facilitate drying wet gear. The mesh stops just before the pry bar fitting.

The larger bin allows for the storage of equipment that needs protection from the elements while the smaller bin is for equipment that can get wet. The black bands with the teeth are fan belts for the engines. In practice, the large storage box often overflowed with personnel gear, food, and sundry items, but rarely ammunition.

The top of the box features duel hinges to allow access to contents in the two bins. The smaller rear hinge folds back onto the larger one, and access to the larger bin requires both tops to be opened.

On vehicles fitted with stowage bins, a guard rail was mounted atop the engine deck to prevent the main gun from firing into the bin. The rail can be seen on this display vehicle, which lacks the storage bin.

Brackets are fitted on the rear hull to hold spare tracks. The first style of bracket consisted of two sets of hooks upon which the tracks can be hung. The upper hooks are fixed. Another, removable set of brackets held the tracks in place where the bolt holes are seen on this particular vehicle.

Brackets are welded to the hull. The moveable clip is held in place by two bolts.

The second type of bracket used. The tracks slid vertically into a lower bracket and were held in place by a retaining clip at the top.

The final type of bracket holds the tracks horizontally by their track pins. The upper clip would be unfastened to release the tracks. Extra track links allowed the crew to replace damaged tracks fairly easily, although great strength was often required.

Although this tank features a guard rail, screens have not yet been attached to this M5A1 undergoing restoration. At the rear are covers on both sides for the fuel and radiator tanks, with the fuel covers being on the outside.

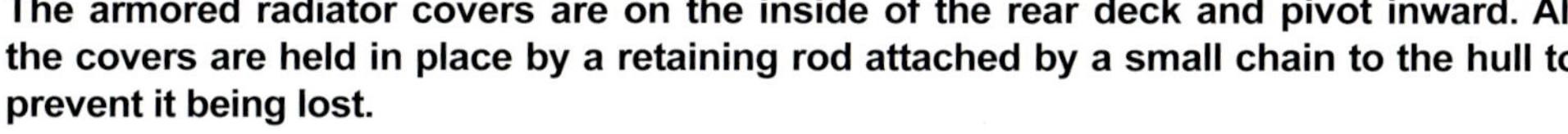

The armored radiator covers are on the inside of the rear deck and pivot inward. All the covers are held in place by a retaining rod attached by a small chain to the hull to prevent it being lost.

This is the layout of the tool storage atop the engine compartment. An axe head, its handle, and wrench are all held down by canvas and leather straps. The covers below them are for the radiator.

The cap on the radiator is similar to that used on cars. There are two cover styles, the most common being the dome-shaped ones shown in these photos. The radiator cap was lifted off by raising the handle and turning the cap.

The armored gas covers, which open at a 45° angle to the side of the hull, are slightly larger than the radiator covers. This cover lacks its retaining pin.

Just forward of the front screen on the right side is a metal hood covering the fire extinguisher handle. To activate the extinguisher from the outside, a soldier simply had to pull on the handle under the hood. This was the only handle on the outside of the tank and allowed a soldier to stop a fire if the crew was disabled or killed by enemy fire.

The top of the gas tank is flush with the surface of the engine deck. The gas cap has a different shape from the radiator cap and is opened by twisting the handles in a counter-clockwise motion.

When the red handle was pulled, the extinguisher was set off in the engine compartment. Because of their gasoline-powered engines and the fact that their main fuel tanks were on the outside of the engine compartment, M5s were easily susceptible to fire.

Bolted to the rear hull on the left is a back-up light.

Bolted to the right side is the blackout light for night driving.

Access to the rear engine compartment is through two sets of double doors that hinge on either side of the engine compartment. This is a late-model rear hull, on which the exhaust deflectors are split by the towing pintle.

The doors open accordion style from the center. The open doors give the crew limited access to the engines. This hull, which lacks the late-model storage box, illustrates how much easier it is to access the compartment when no box is attached.

The doors can fold back on themselves, or fold outward as one unit. The rod on the door keeps the door from hitting the exhaust pipe.

Dual exhaust pipes carry engine gases down and away from the engine compartment. The addition of the exhaust deflectors helped reduce the amount of dust and debris kicked up by the exhaust and radiators. Such refuse could reveal a tank's position.

In late 1943 a towing pintle was added to the M5 series. This was capable of pulling a 5-ton armored ammunition or fuel trailer.

At the time the towing pintle was added, the M5 was equipped with exhaust deflectors. Adding the pintle required the splitting of the lower exhaust deflector. The door hinges are very substantial because of the weight of the doors. (Duane Ward)

Piping exhaust to the left side of each screen substantially reduced the amount of dust and debris kicked up when the engines were running. (Duane Ward)

The pintle is attached to a mount and held in place by four bolts. The mount itself is welded to the lower rear hull. (Bill Klingbeil)

Heavy-duty mounts are welded at the bottom of the rear hull. These are designed for mounting tow shackles or for tying down the vehicle during transportation. The extensive weld beads gave these mounts great strength. Mounts rarely failed. (Bill Klingbeil)

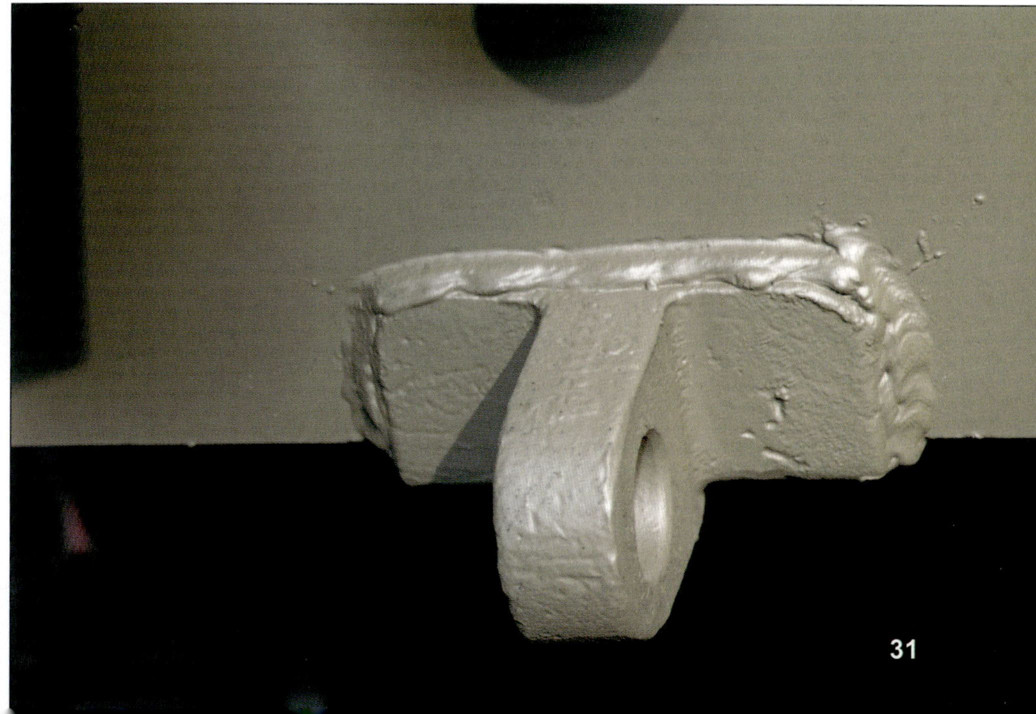

These photos show the general hull layout with the turret removed. Looking forward, the driver's compartment is to the left while the assistant driver's position is to the right.

On the bottom of the right side is the assistant driver's seat and directly behind it is the floor escape hatch. (Bill Klingbeil)

On the right side of the hull is the 37mm ammunition rack. It appears in the center of this photo, flanked on either side by racks for the machine gun ammunition. (Bill Klingbeil)

There are more machine gun ammunition racks on the left side of the hull. Additional ammo boxes were carried inside the hull or strapped on the outside. (Bill Klingbeil)

On the lower left side of the hull is the driver's seat, directly behind which is the battery box. Dividing the compartment in half are the dual drive shafts. The assistant driver sits to the right of the drive shafts. (Bill Klingbeil)

At the bottom of the rear of the compartment are the attachments for the drive train from the hydramatic transmission to the front of the hull. Visible under the drive train are the round covers for the axles. (Bill Klingbeil)

At the rear of the compartment is the firewall. The dual Cadillac engines are clearly visible, since the doors in the firewall have not been attached.

The hull roof had two supports for the turret ring. The supports are attached to the roller housing and welded to a flange that is welded to the hull interior side. Extensive welding eliminated the need for bolts used on earlier tanks. Bolts sheared off under the impact of enemy fire to become deadly pieces of shrapnel ricocheting around inside the hull.

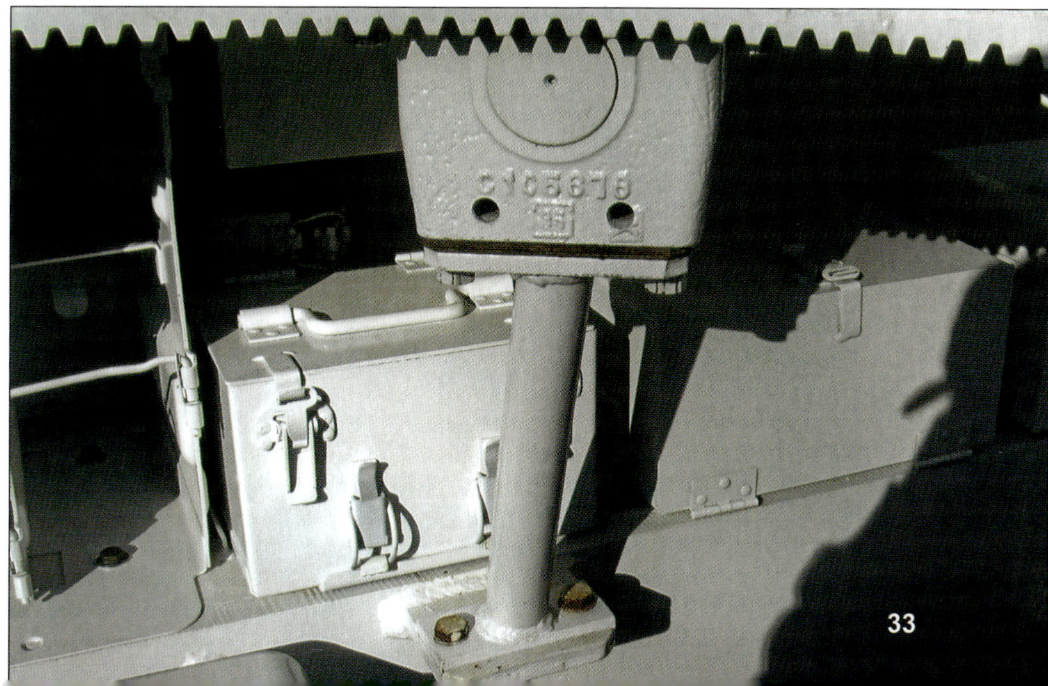

The teeth of the turret ring are easily discernible in this view from inside the compartment, looking up past the right front section of the hull. The rectangular box is the housing for the turret roller. The shaft extending downward is for support.

The three rollers set 120° apart in the turret ring allow the turret to traverse easily and smoothly. The turret roller housing can be seen under the teeth of the turret ring.

The transfer unit is located between the drivers' seats. It is attached to the final drive in the front of the tank.

The couplings from the propeller shaft to the transfer unit can be seen on either side of the support pole. They transmitted power from the twin Cadillac engines in the rear to the transmission.

With the turret removed, details of the drivers' compartment become readily visible. The springs to the left of the seat facilitate raising and lowering the seat.

The drivers' seats were two-piece affairs with a metal form for the seat and a removable back. Black leather pads were attached to these. The back plate has not been attached to the assistant driver's seat seen below. Part of the escape hatch is visible at the right.

The double spring assembly allows the seat to be raised or lowered with minimum effort. The seat can be raised high enough to allow the driver's head to be above the top of the hull when seated. This is the assistant driver's seat. (Bill Klingbeil)

The entire assistant driver's seat is seen through the hatch from directly overhead. The object next the upper left corner of the seat (at the bottom of the photo) is the grip of the .30 caliber machine gun. (Duane Ward)

The driver's position appears in this view from directly behind the driver's seat. The accelerator pedal is just below the instrument panel.

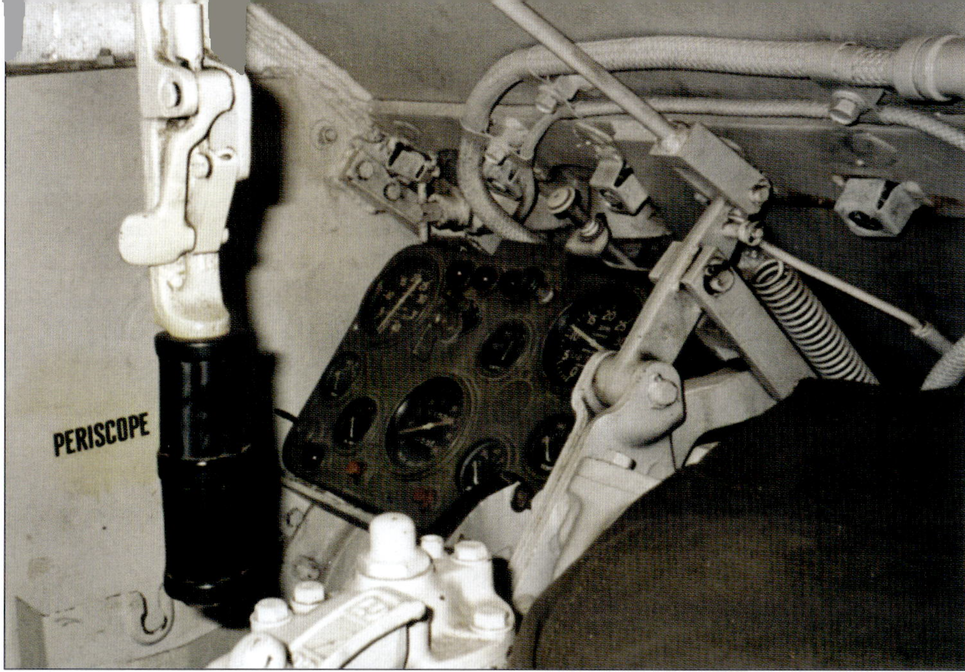

The driver's position is seen in this view over the transfer unit from the assistant driver's position. The levers are the steering and brake mechanism. There are dual controls for both drivers.

Driver's Compartment

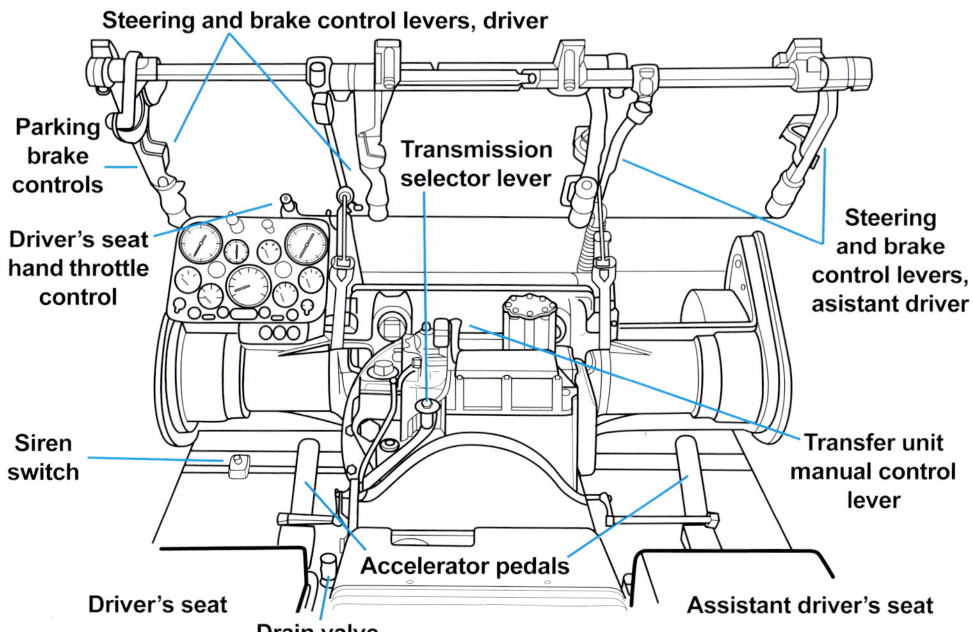

The steering and brake levers are similar in design and are operated by releasing the small lever above the handle. This action allows the driver to move the lever to the desired position on the half-moon gear located at the top.

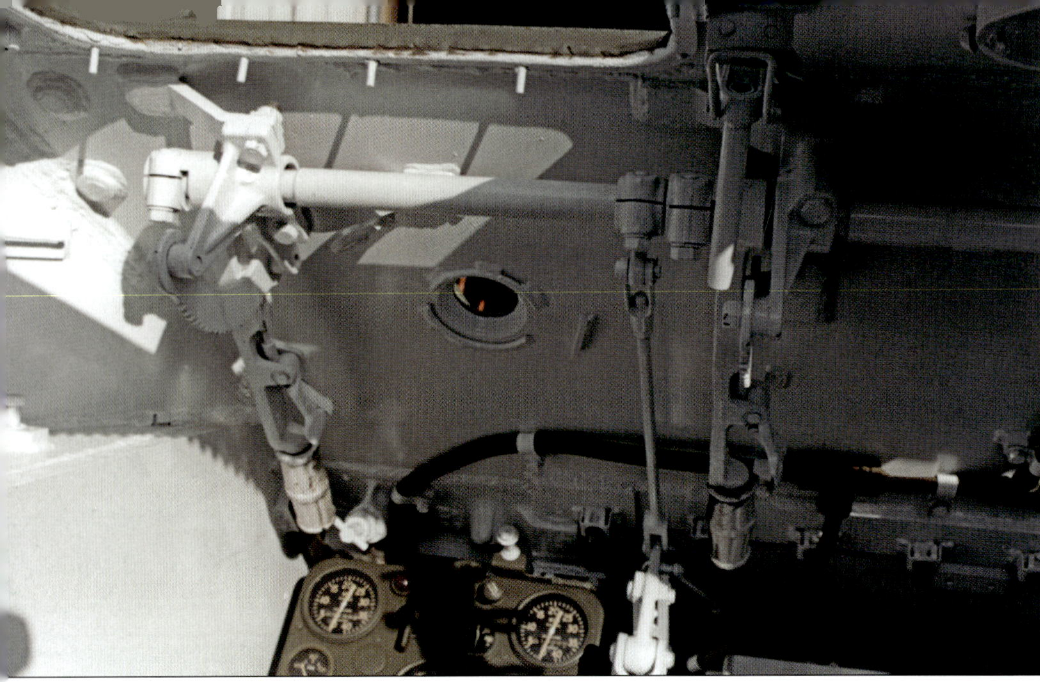

The steering and braking controls are mounted on a rod that extends across the top of the glacis plate. The rod connects the controls to both the drivers' positions.

The gearshift lever is located to the right of the driver. The curved handle allows the assistant driver easier access to it. If the driver were wounded or killed, the assistant driver could take over but it was much more difficult for him to operate the vehicle from his position on the right side. (Duane Ward)

The braking and steering unit is similar to that used on the M18 "Hellcat." This photograph shows how it is mounted to the top of the glacis plate over the assistant driver's position.

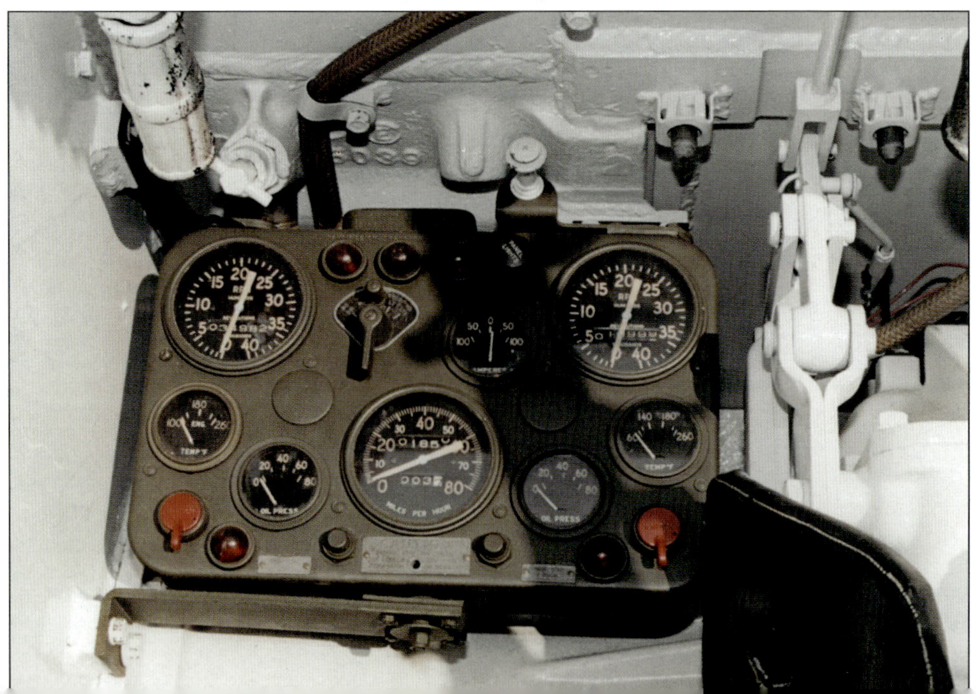

Tachometers for the two engines are located in the upper corners of the driver's instrument panel. Gauges showing temperature and oil pressure for each engine are in the lower corners of the instrument panel. The speedometer is located in the center.

For indirect viewing, each driver's position has an M6 periscope that rotates 360° and swivels up and down.

Damaged periscope components could easily be replaced from spares kept onboard the vehicle. The periscope eyepiece is removed by loosening a knob on the front of the housing. Just below the periscope is a small direct-vision port into which a protective plug has been inserted. The chain attached to the plug facilitates pulling the plug into place.

The plugs that cover the small direct vision ports for both drivers are chained to the inside of the tank. When the crew buttoned up, they pulled the plug back into place. To push the plug out again, the rectangular fitting was slipped into a vertical position, which allowed the plug to slide out. The small port afforded an extremely limited field of view, basically confined to a small arc immediately in front of the tank.

The final drive runs across the front of the driver's compartment and bolts into the side of the hull. The transfer power case is just visible to the right.

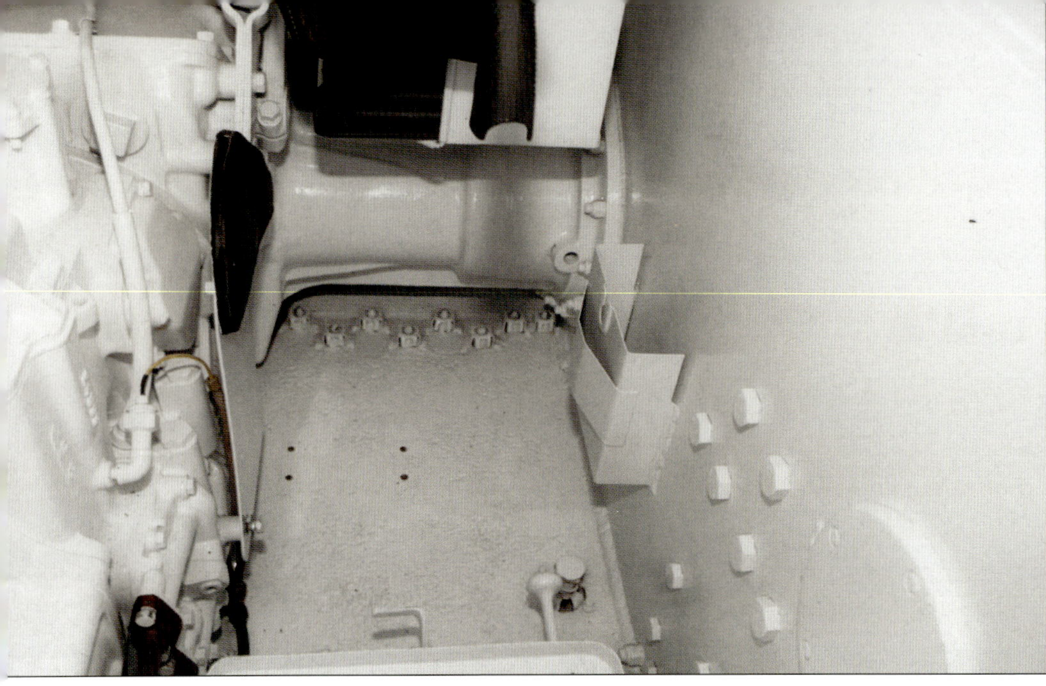

The two final drive housings are mirror images of each other. The bolts on the right side hold the bogie wheel unit in place.

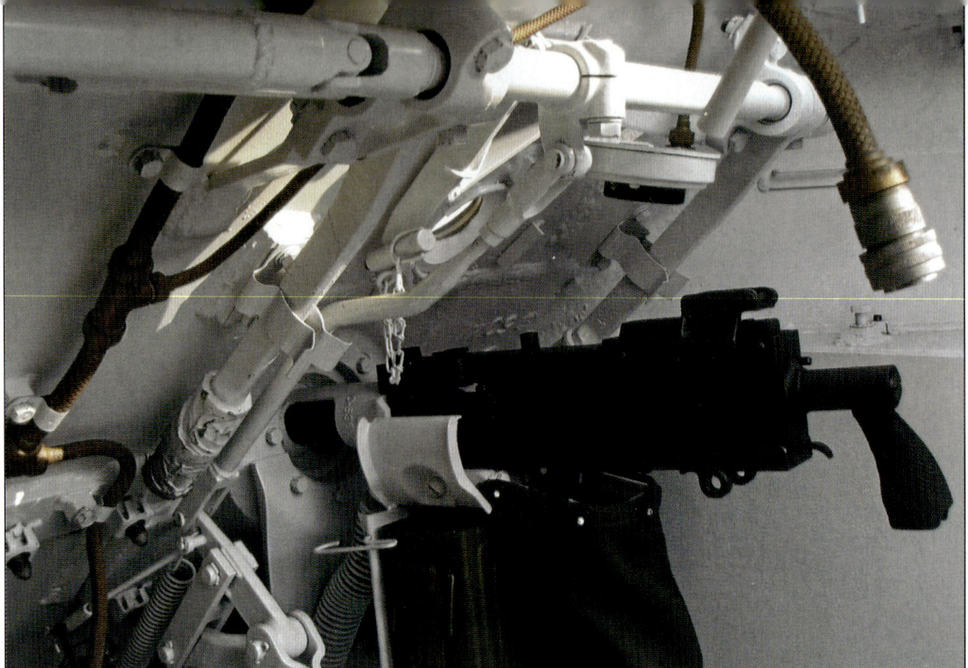

The assistant driver was responsible for operating the .30 caliber machine gun, shown here from the vantage point of the driver's seat. This weapon was used for general suppression fire while the tank approached a target.

The machine gun was fed from an ammunition box attached under the gun. A canvas bag was fitted under the gun to catch ejected shell casings, preventing them from scattering around the interior.them.

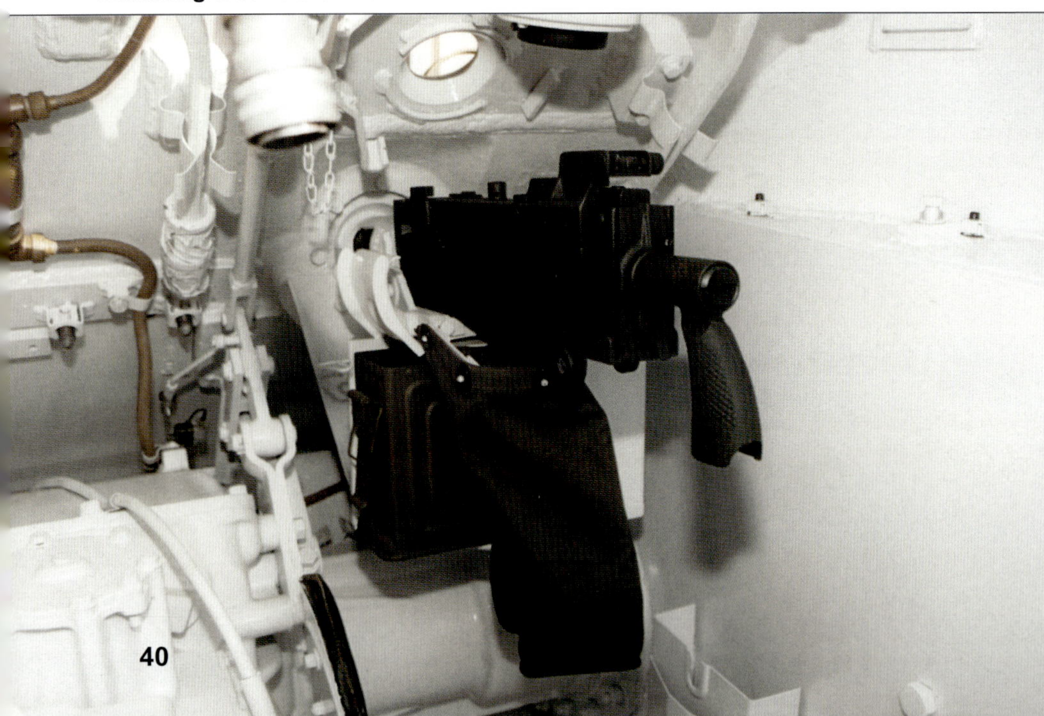

The ball mount appears without the machine gun, ammo case and bag fitted. The curved fitting just to the left of the opening is a guide from the ammunition belt. (Bill Klingbeil)

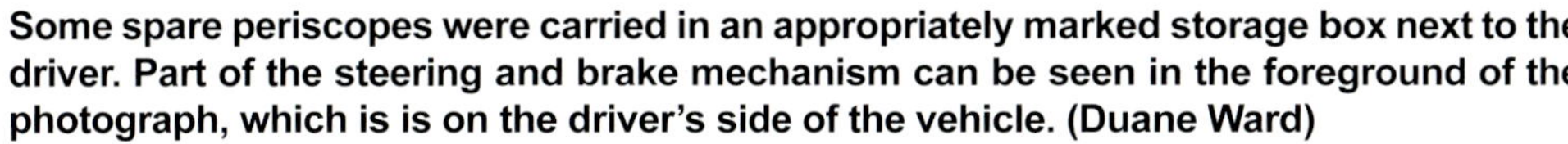

Some spare periscopes were carried in an appropriately marked storage box next to the driver. Part of the steering and brake mechanism can be seen in the foreground of the photograph, which is is on the driver's side of the vehicle. (Duane Ward)

With the turret in place, the drivers' positions are cramped. The driver's position is seen here, looking down from the left side of the turret. (Duane Ward)

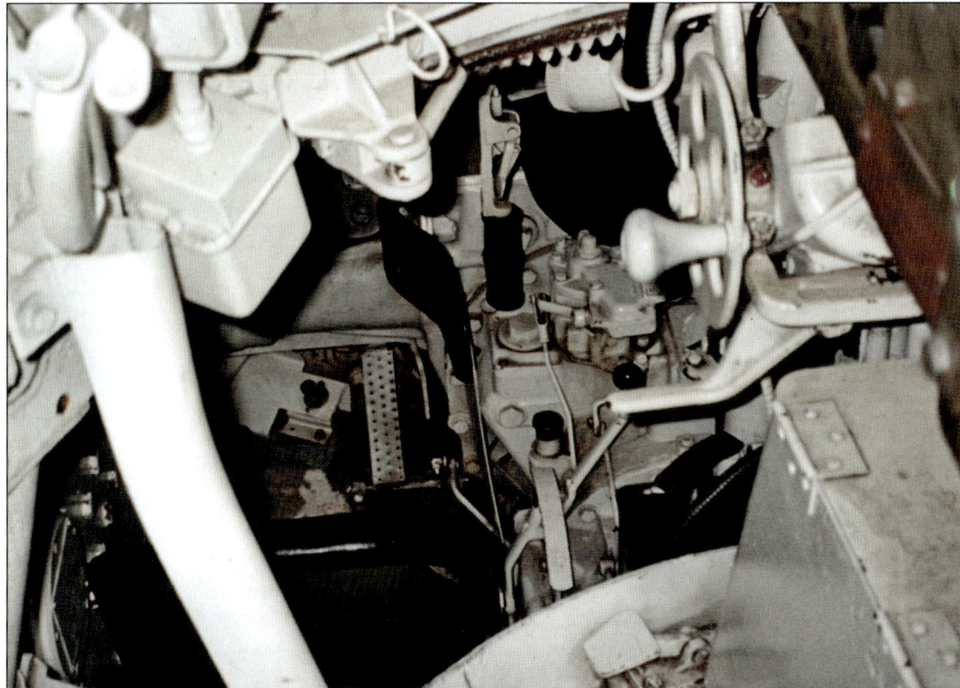

Across from the driver, an identical periscope stowage box sits next to the assistant driver. Behind the box is a rack for .30 caliber ammunition cans. (Duane Ward)

Also cramped is the assistant driver's position, seen here from the right side of the turret. The size of the M5 meant that its personnel could not be large men. But even for small men in combat gear, the M5 interior was a tight fit. (Duane Ward)

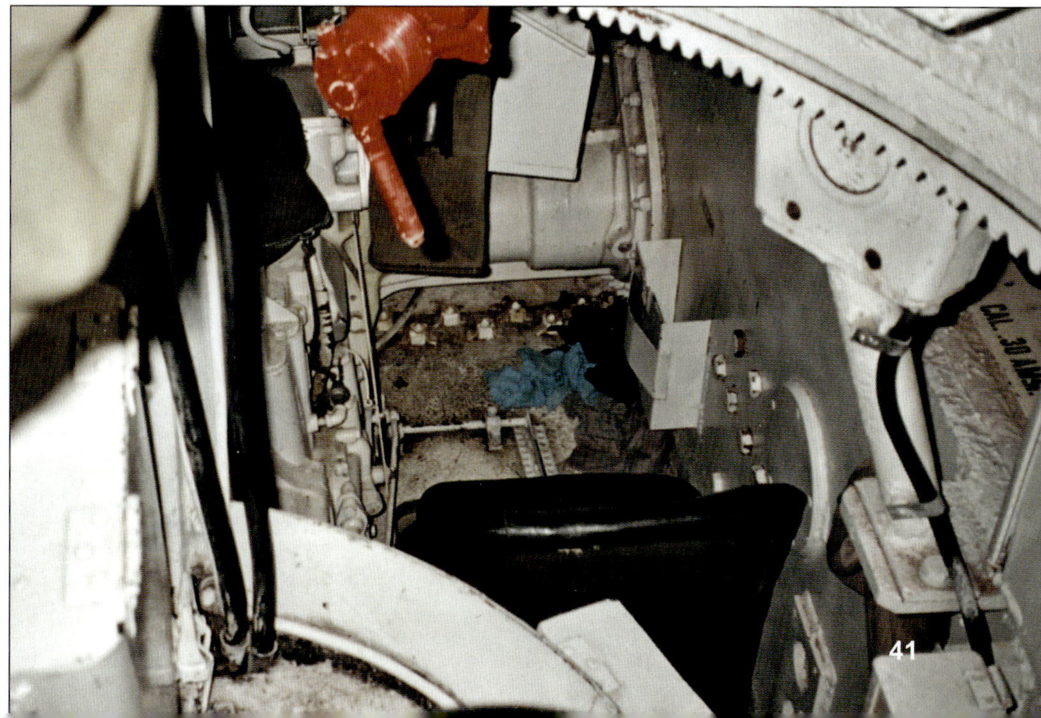

The trapezoidal escape hatch, located behind the assistant driver's seat, was introduced in the late 1942. There was no escape hatch in the floor of early M5s.

Just behind the .30 caliber rack is a stowage bin for the 37mm ammunition. Raising the handle opened the double doors. (Duane Ward)

The .30 caliber ammunition rack next to the assistant driver held six boxes in two rows of three. The M5 carried 6,250 rounds of .30 caliber ammunition. (Duane Ward)

This rack held 24 rounds of 37mm ammunition. The M5 carried 123 and the M5A1 carried 147 rounds of 37mm ammunition in a combination of ready racks and storage boxes.

The 37mm rounds were held in place by these clips that secured the lip on the bottom of the shell. (Bill Klingbeil)

There is another .30 caliber ammunition rack behind the 37mm rack. The total number of .30 caliber rounds carried by the M5A1 was 6,750.

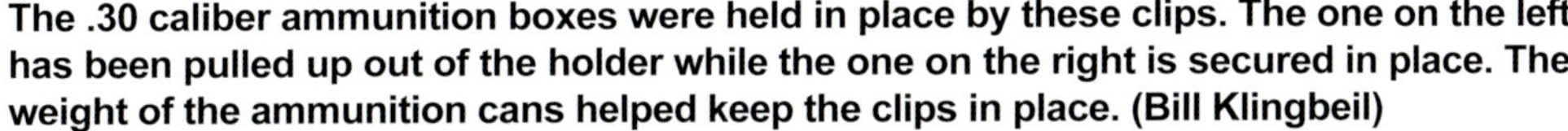

The .30 caliber ammunition boxes were held in place by these clips. The one on the left has been pulled up out of the holder while the one on the right is secured in place. The weight of the ammunition cans helped keep the clips in place. (Bill Klingbeil)

This .30 caliber rack on the left side of the hull held 12 ammunition boxes. Experience showed that the M5 used far more .30 caliber machine gun ammunition than 37mm ammunition and the crews carried as much of it as possible, when going into action.

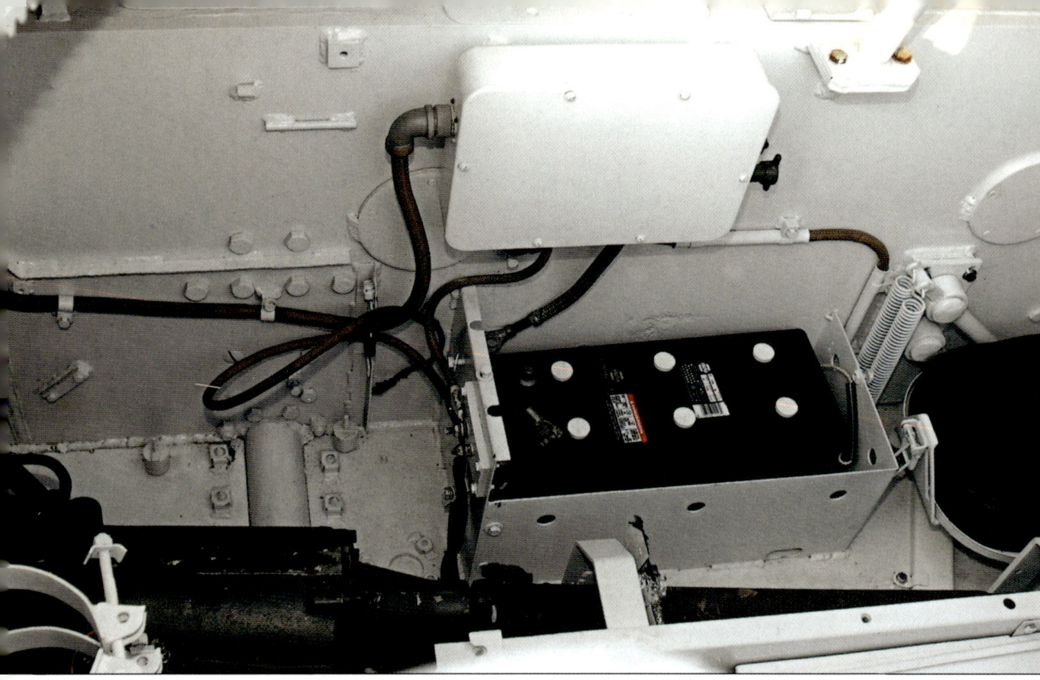

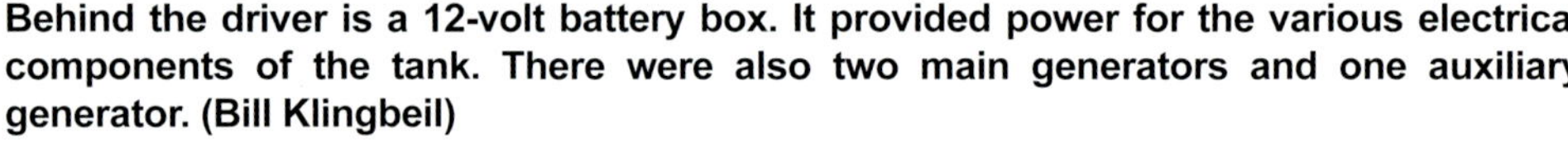

Behind the driver is a 12-volt battery box. It provided power for the various electrical components of the tank. There were also two main generators and one auxiliary generator. (Bill Klingbeil)

The top of the lid slides back, since the bottom of the turret basket, when it was in place, restricted access to the stowage container.

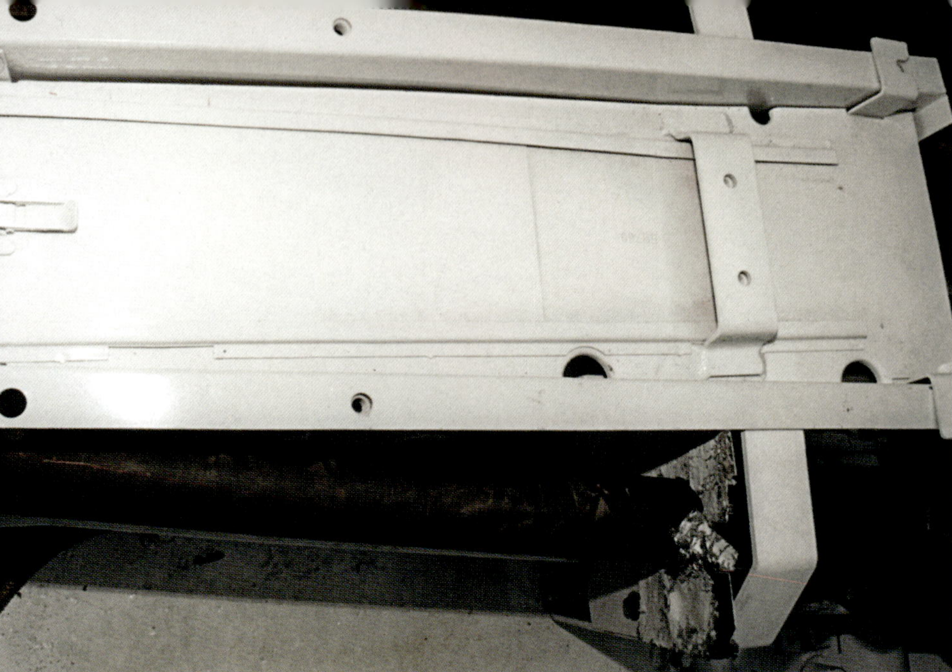

Between the drive shafts is a small storage container for various items of gear. With the turret basket in place, this bin is difficult to access.

The twin Cadillac engines are mounted on either side of the engine compartment. Their transmissions extend under the firewall into the crew compartment. The shafts to the front drive sprockets run down through the middle of the compartment.

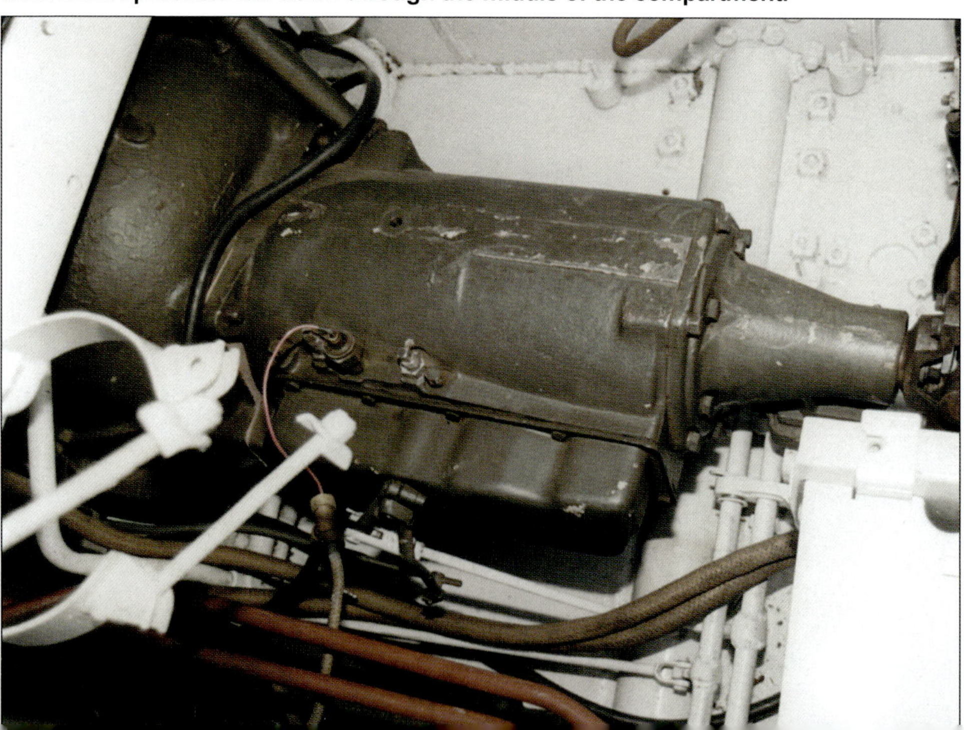

Looking through the firewall at the engine on the right, exhaust pipes and a distributor cap are easily distinguishable. The left engine is a mirror image of that on the right. The small oval object to the left of the distributor cap is the nozzle for the fire extinguisher.

The fighting compartment is seen from above with all the covers and additional ammunition boxes in place. When compared with earlier photos, the cramped conditions of the compartment are very evident.

The transmissions are covered by sheet metal boxes, atop which are two bins for 37mm ammunition. Between them is the engine compartment's fire extinguisher, which contained 10 pounds of carbon dioxide. (Bill Klingbeil)

Each bin held 55 rounds of 37mm ammunition. The two-piece hatch folds back for access to the bin. Though there was a prescribed ammunition list, actual ammo varied, depending on the expected combat conditions. (Bill Klingbeil)

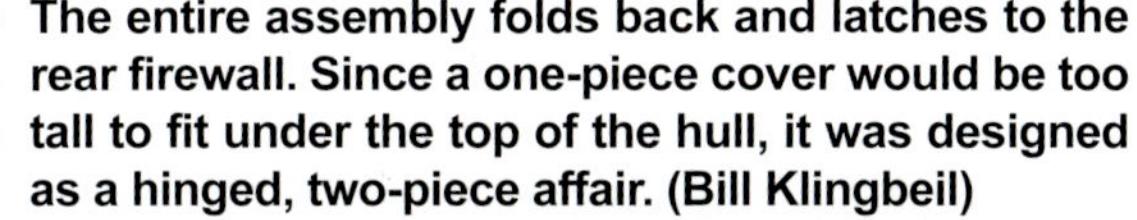

The entire assembly folds back and latches to the rear firewall. Since a one-piece cover would be too tall to fit under the top of the hull, it was designed as a hinged, two-piece affair. (Bill Klingbeil)

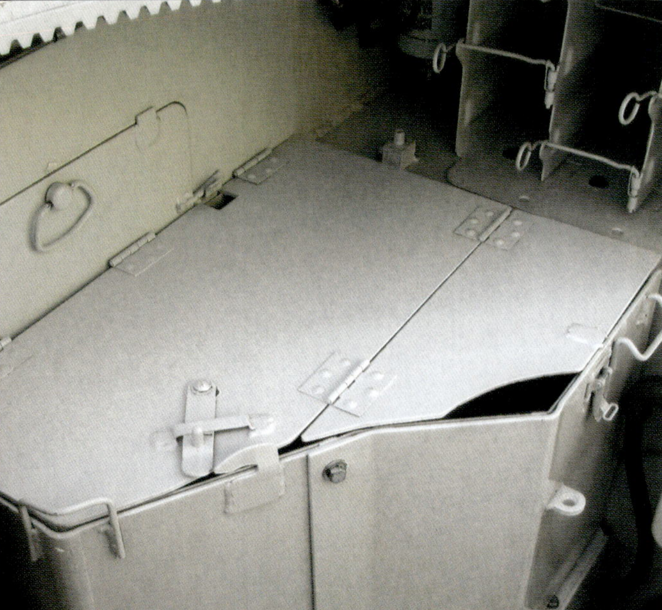

This engine has been pulled out for maintenance and is hanging from a hoist. The transmission housing is on the lower left. The long rectangular box on the upper right below the radiator pipe covers the spark plugs. There are four spark plugs on either side of the engine. (Lance Miller)

Engine / Radiator

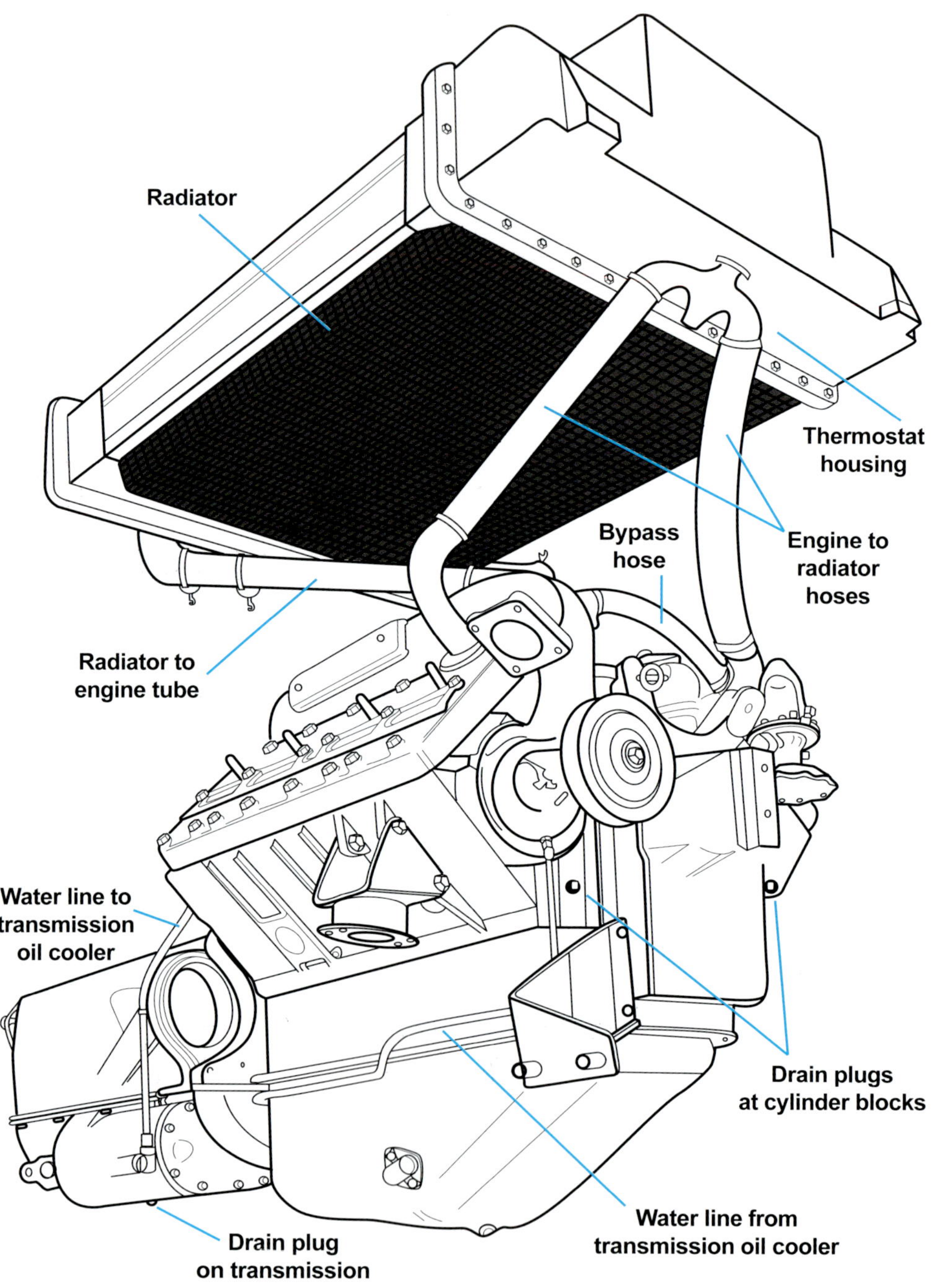

In this view of the underside of the engine, the exhaust pipe is at the top and the lower portion of the transmission cover is at the bottom. The engine oil pan is located between them. (Lance Miller)

Under the deck, above the engines, are the radiators, viewed here looking towards the rear of the vehicle. The caps for filling the radiators are on the small boxes at the top. Access to the caps is through armored covers on the engine deck. (Jim Hess)

In this overhead view of the engine compartment with the radiators removed, the turret ring is to the right while the engine access doors are on the left. The tubes sticking up next to the doors are for the radiators. (Lance Miller)

The white tube in the upper left is from the fuel tank and goes in through the carburetor underneath it. The radiator hose is seen at the bottom. Also apparent are various linkages that connect the two engines. (Lance Miller)

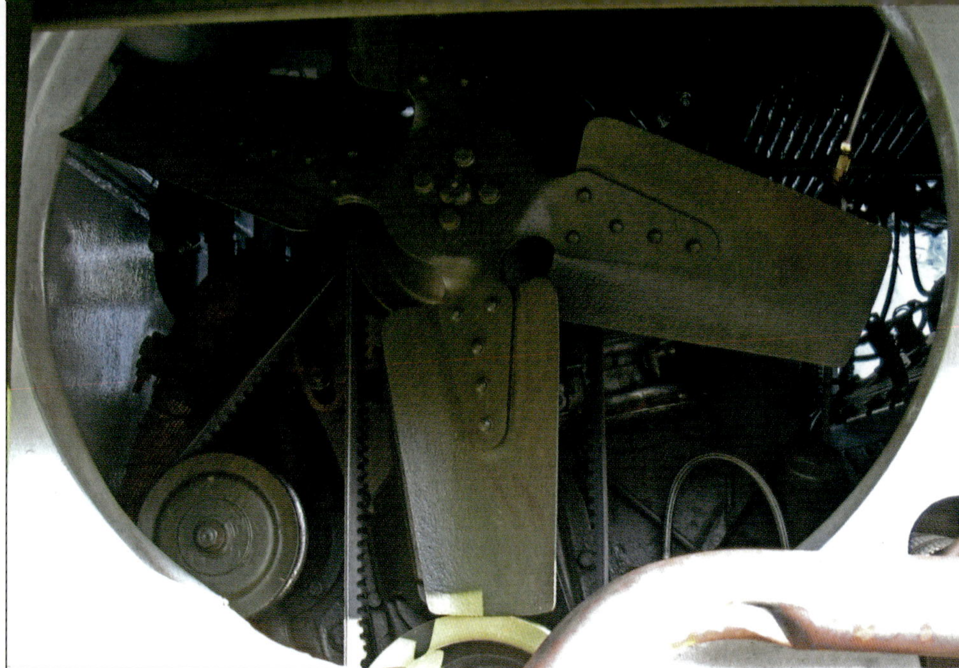

With the rear plate in place, the view inside the engine compartment is restricted, especially with the fan mounted. The water pump is mounted right behind the small fly wheel on the left.

The two engines are seen from behind with the rear engine plate removed. The engine fans have been removed from the large top wheel on each engine. Clearly visible are the thick teeth on the fan belts. (Jim Hess)

M5 Longitudinal Cross Section

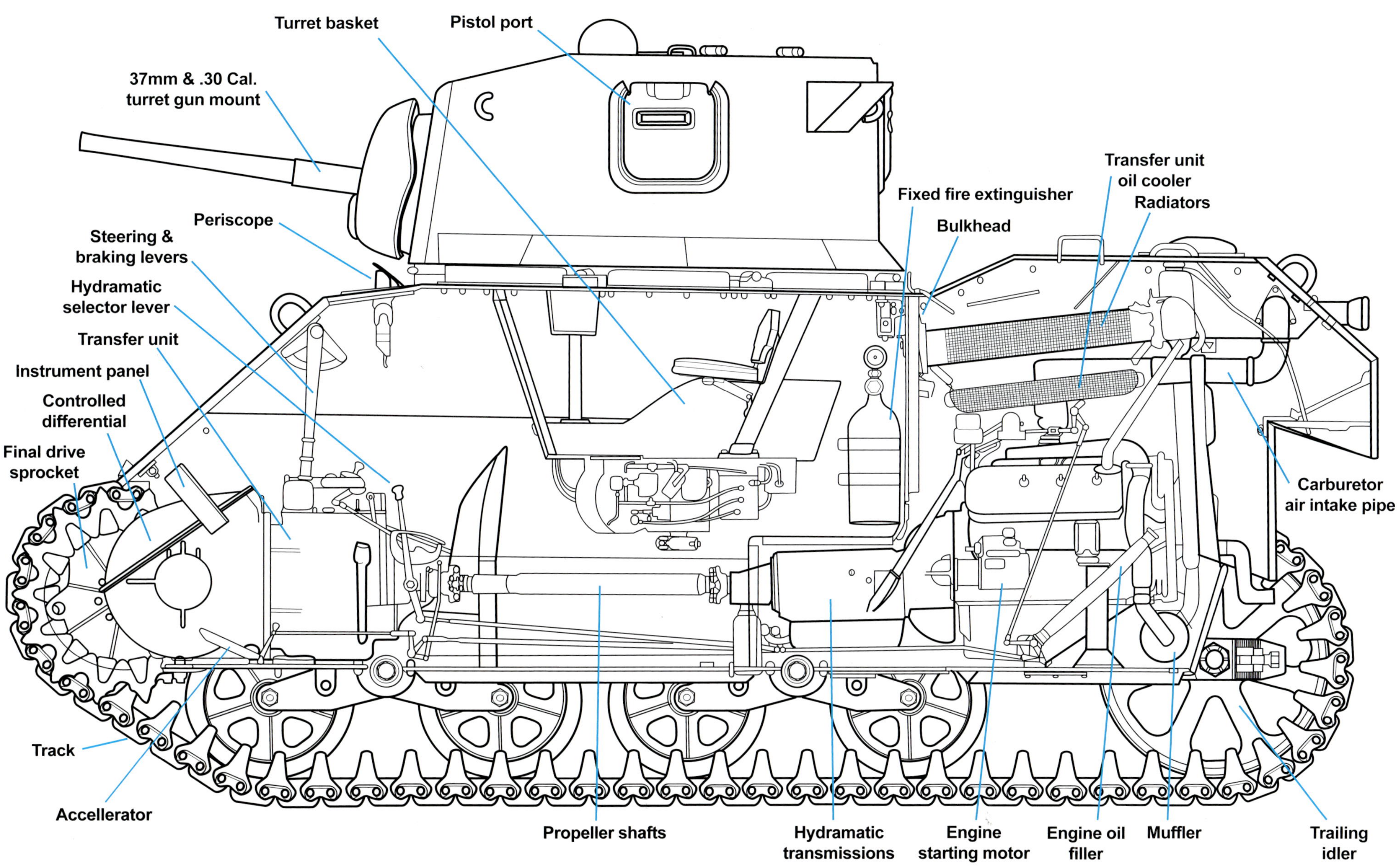

Like late-model M3 turrets, the early M5 turrets feature pistol ports on both sides and at the rear. Grouser brackets were welded to the sides of most M5 turrets, though a few examples lacked them.

The antenna mount is a simple bracket welded to the turret side. Unlike the M5A1 with a radio mounted in the turret bustle, the M5 radio was mounted in the hull. (Gary Binder)

Among the features of the M5 turret are an antenna mount behind the gunner's position and a telescoping mount for a .30 caliber machine gun behind the commander's position. (Gary Binder)

The pistol ports on the turret proved to be of limited value and eventually were deleted from later versions of the series. (Gary Binder)

M5 turret features triangular hatches for both the commander and gunner. This early M5 features the one-piece engine deck. (PAM)

Hatches can fold on top of one another. The gunner had a fixed M4 periscope while the commander's M6 periscope could rotate 360°. (PAM)

The turret for the M5 was adapted from the M3A1 and features hatches for both the commander and gunner. This improved crew access over the original M3 series. (Gary Binder)

The triangular hatches are relatively small and cramped. The arrangement for opening them at the same time was also awkward. Hatches on the later M5A1 series were much roomier and caused no problems when opened. (Gary Binder)

While the front of the M5A1 turret is similar to the that of the M5, the rear is totally different and extends back in a bustle. Both hatches on the M5A1 are squared off and offer much better access than those on the M5. (Bob Steinbrunn)

The 37mm cannon is mounted in a cast gun mantlet, designated M44. The gunner's sight is on the left and has a small cover over the top. The small lip on the side of the housing helps to line up the forward part of the barrel.

M5A Turret

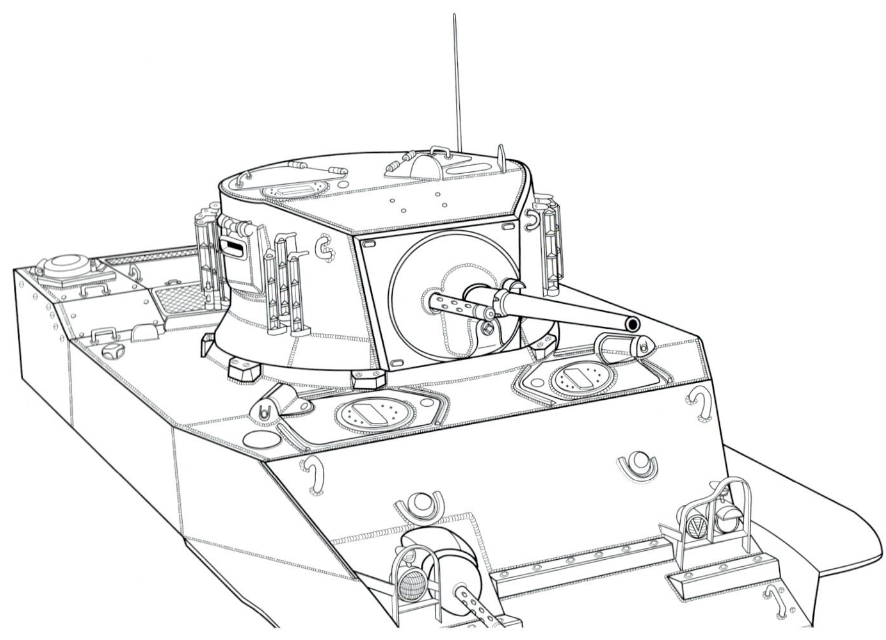

The hatches allow easy access to the turret. The canvas cover at the bottom of the photo conceals the new bustle area for radio mounting in the turret rear. (Duane Ward)

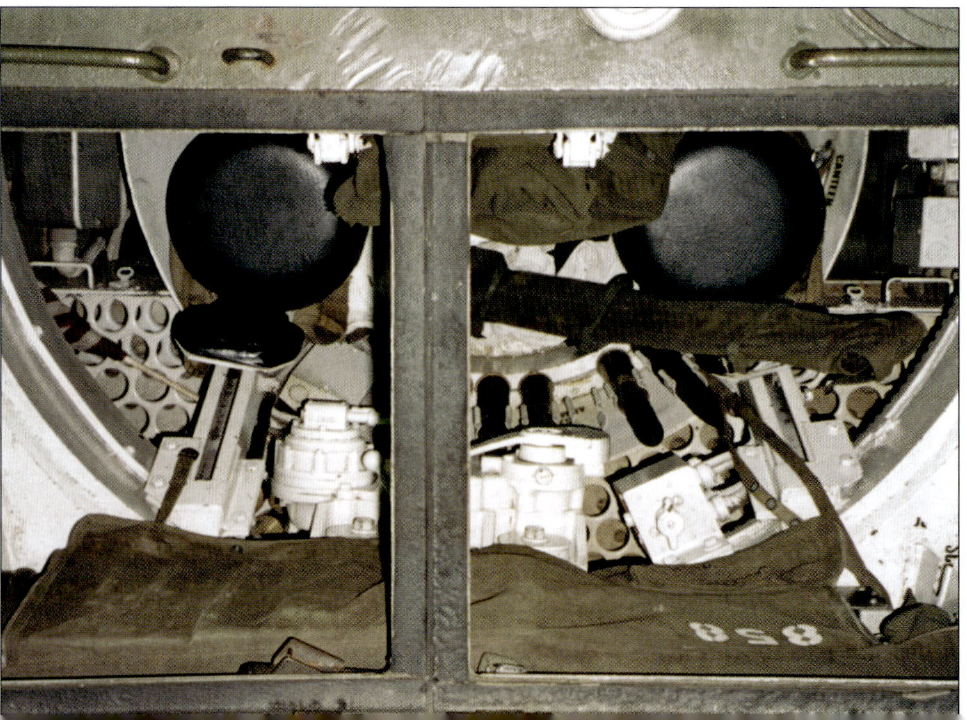

The top of the mantlet has a small edge that varies slightly with manufacture. A .30 caliber machine gun is mounted co-axially with the 37mm cannon.

Early M5A1 Turret

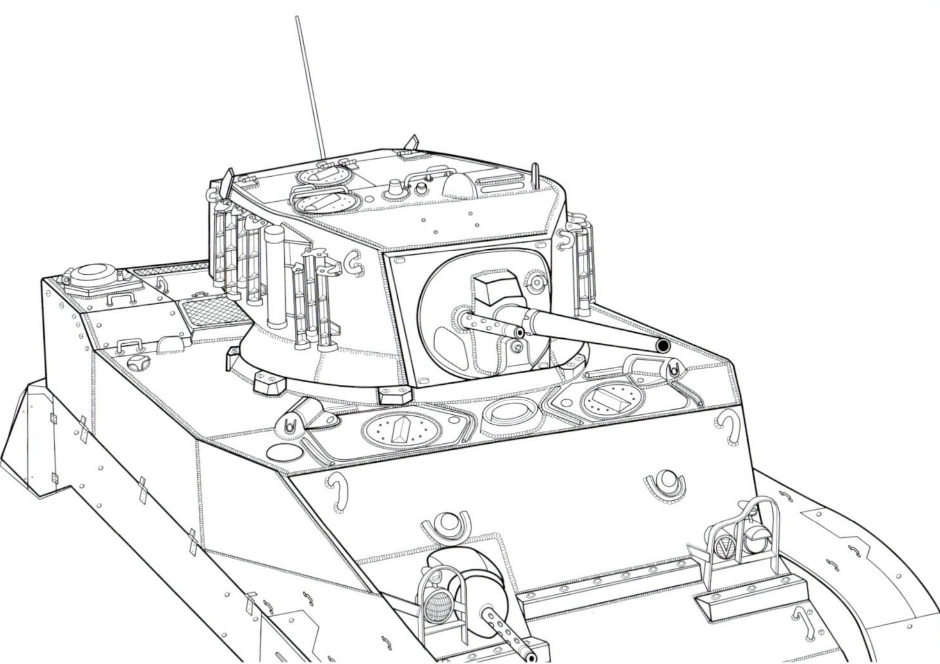

This turret under restoration shows the bulging gun mount without the mantlet. The sight is to the right in the oval-shaped hole. (Bill Klingbeil)

The rectangular cutout on the left is for the co-axial machine gun. The barrel has not been screwed into the main part of the gun assembly. (Bill Klingbeil)

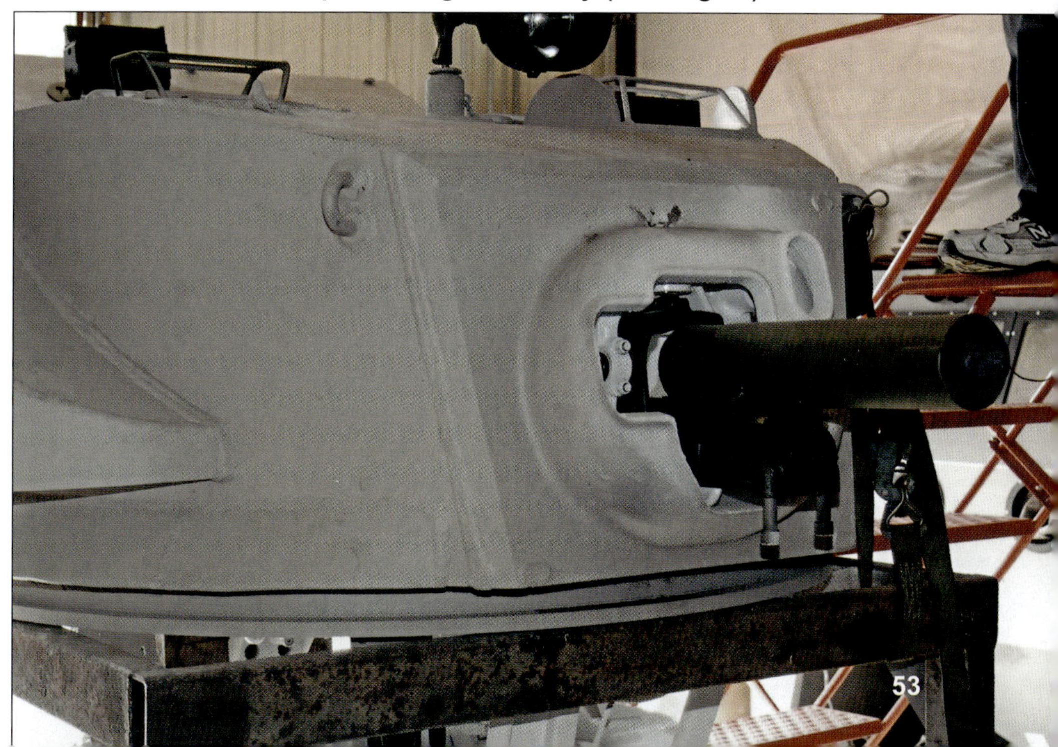

Pistol ports were welded shut after they proved to be of little use and to lessen the structural strength of the turret. (Rob Ervin)

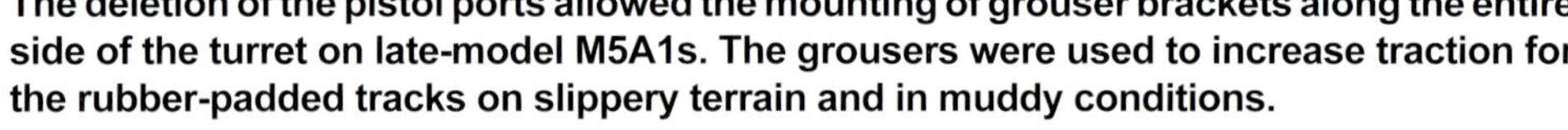

The deletion of the pistol ports allowed the mounting of grouser brackets along the entire side of the turret on late-model M5A1s. The grousers were used to increase traction for the rubber-padded tracks on slippery terrain and in muddy conditions.

On later-manufactured turrets, the pistol ports are completely eliminated, and no trace of them remains.

Late M5A1 Turret

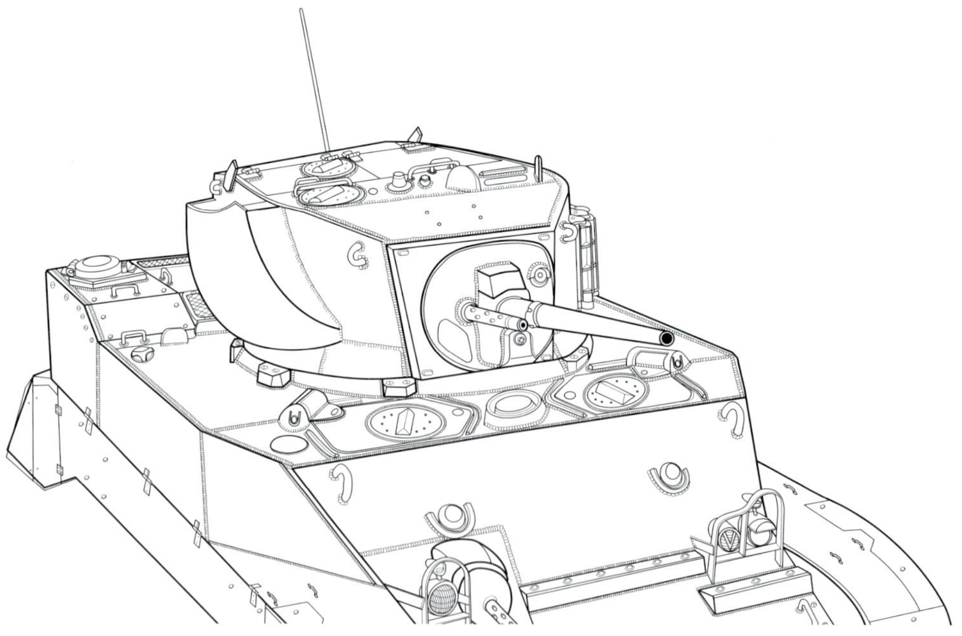

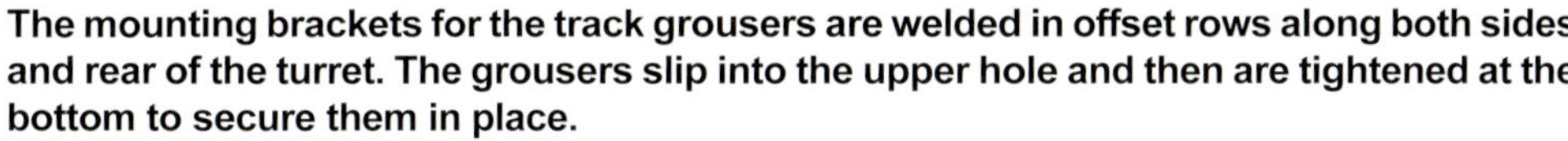

The mounting brackets for the track grousers are welded in offset rows along both sides and rear of the turret. The grousers slip into the upper hole and then are tightened at the bottom to secure them in place.

The grousers are slipped into the holes on the top two sets of brackets and hang down in alternating rows. (Bob Steinbrunn)

One end of the grouser is removable. When hung in brackets, the removable grouser end is bolted back to the grouser through the bottom bracket to secure it. (Bob Steinbrunn)

Grousers help give added traction in mud and icy conditions. The outside of the grouser is designed to grip whatever surface it comes in contact with. The inside is smooth. At both ends of the grouser are connecting points.

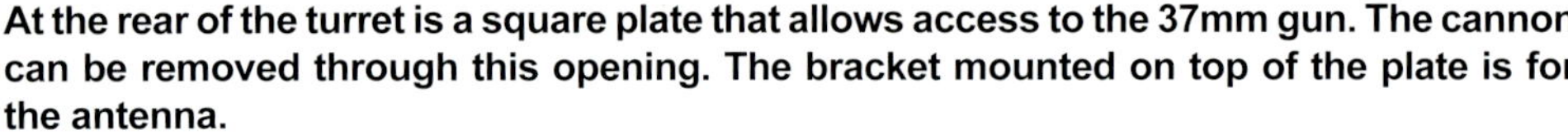

At the rear of the turret is a square plate that allows access to the 37mm gun. The cannon can be removed through this opening. The bracket mounted on top of the plate is for the antenna.

The antenna bracket would be seated in the hole on the antenna base. The base, in turn, is welded to the access plate on the rear of the turret. On both sides of the antenna bracket are brackets with holes that were used for hanging track grousers. (Bill Klingbeil)

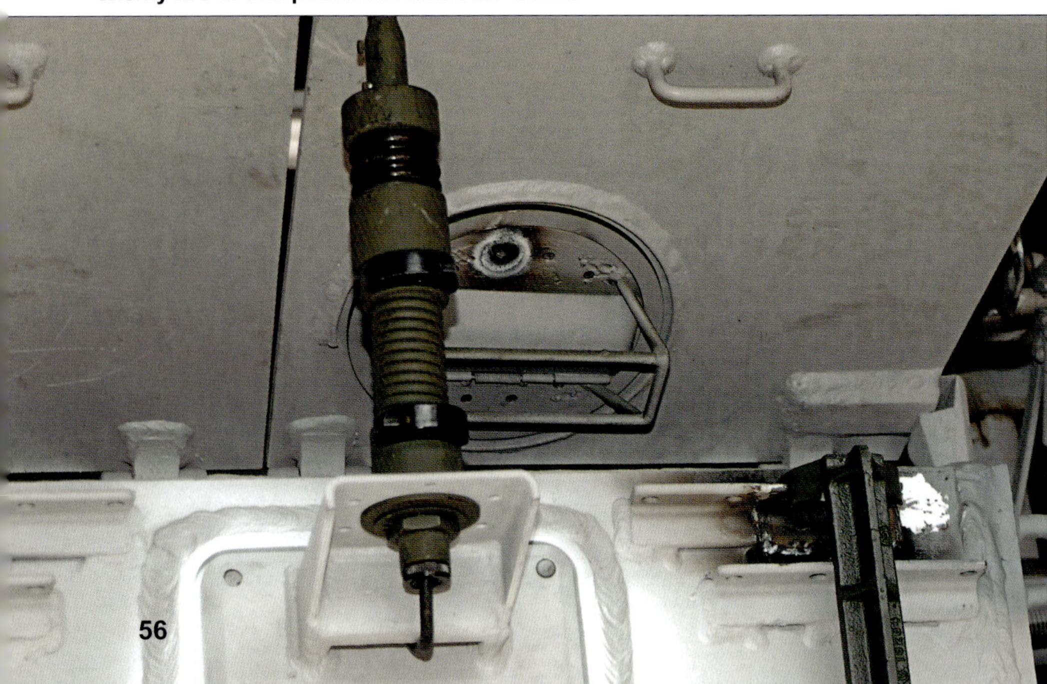

The antenna is here bolted onto the bracket. A wire runs from the antenna base into the turret to the radio through a small hole on the plate. The wire is fairly well protected from enemy fire in this position behind the turret.

The path for the wire from the antenna to the radio inside the turret bustle is seen here from underneath. The offset arrangement of the grouser brackets is also evident. To the far right is the underside of the armored machine gun mount.

Both the commander and gunner have their own hatches that swing up and to the rear. Only the commander's hatch has a periscope, not mounted in this photo. The handle on the gunner's turret is for locking the hatch in the open position. The handle for the commander's hatch has not been fitted. (Bill Klingbeil)

The commander has two periscopes while the gunner has one. Periscopes are protected by small metal flaps and wire guards. The hatches are held in place by locking brackets welded to the turret on both sides of the hatches. (Bill Klingbeil)

When the hatch is open, a small pin fits into a receptacle on the side of the turret.

The hatches swing up and to the rear and rest on flanges welded to the side of the turret.

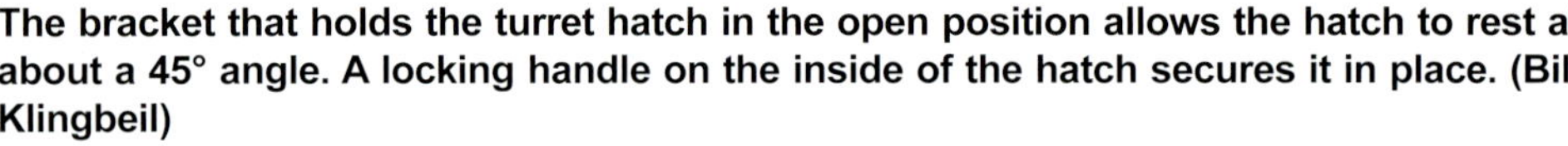

The bracket that holds the turret hatch in the open position allows the hatch to rest at about a 45° angle. A locking handle on the inside of the hatch secures it in place. (Bill Klingbeil)

Two sets of latches on the front of the turret roof hold the hatches closed. Rods pull the latches onto the locking points of the hatches. (Bill Klingbeil)

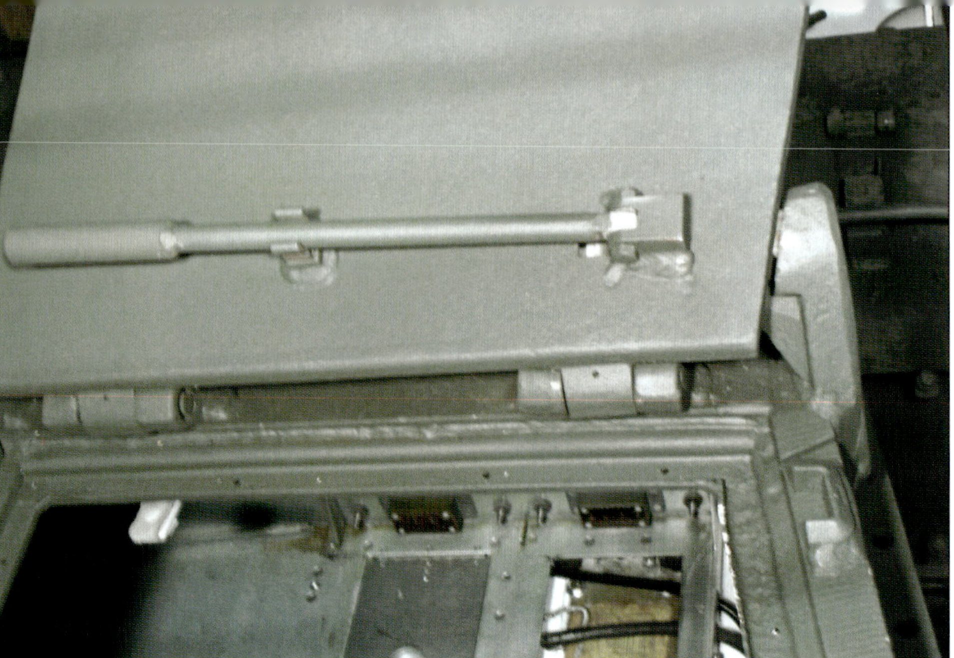

The handle for locking the hatch in the open position is mounted in brackets on the turret roof. The handle pushes a small metal locking pin into the brackets to secure the hatch in the upright position.

The heavy bracket that holds the hatch in the open position is welded to the turret adjacent to the hatch.

The external .30 caliber machine gun is on a telescoping M20 mount behind the tank commander's hatch on the M5, an awkward arrangement necessitated by the pistol ports on the side of the turret. (PAM)

With the elimination of the pistol ports on later turret models, the machine gun mount was moved forward to a less-awkward position on the side, and slightly in front, of the tank commander.

Locating the machine gun mount just behind the front grouser storage point made it accessible for the commander, but also greatly exposed to enemy fire. Japanese snipers took advantage of dense Pacific foliage to pick off exposed tank commanders manning the machine gun.

The post for the machine gun mount is welded to two brackets that are bolted to the side of the turret. To counter the effects of vibration from the machine gun, the upper bracket is double the size of the lower one and is held in place by four bolts, compared to two on the lower bracket. (Bob Steinbrunn)

In 1943 a new type of machine gun mount, designated D60490, was introduced. This mount folds back into an armored cover, protecting the gun when not in use.

The basic gun cradle remained unchanged, but the D60490 folding mechanism was more complex than the older, telescoping M20 mount. The bracket on the side is for the ammunition box. (Bill Klingbeil)

The most commonly used ammunition box held 250 rounds that were belt fed into the machine gun. Barely visible under the lip of the turret hatch is the locking pin that holds the mount in place. (Bill Klingbeil)

This machine gun and cradle, seen here fitted out with an ammunition box, have been locked down to prevent movement.

Located just under the lip of the turret hatch are the pin and latch for locking the machine gun mount in place. The mount could be fixed in either the up or down position. (Bill Klingbeil)

To hold the cradle in place, a support arm extends up from the main swivel arm to just below the rear of the cradle, where a pin locks it in place. (Bill Klingbeil)

Reliability and high rate of fire make the .30 caliber machine gun, seen here from the right side in its cradle, an excellent weapon for suppression fire.

The entire mount pivots into its protective shield by swiveling down and back. Once in place, the mount can be locked down until needed. Though it appears complex, the mechanism is actually quite simple to operate and very sturdy. (Bill Klingbeil)

A curved shield protecting the machine gun is welded to the right side of the turret on late-production vehicles, which also feature exhaust deflectors and a towing pintle.

The shield conforms to the shape of the side of the turret. It is open on the bottom, although the bottom edge has an added rim that runs part-way around.

Brackets welded at the front and rear of the bottom of the shield provide it additional support. The rim on the shield extends back from the bracket, but not forward of it.

Forward of the front support bracket, the shield lacks a bottom rim. The weld line attaching the shield to the turret can be seen in this view from underneath.

Two bottom brackets help steady the armored shield, which is welded to the turret and open on the back and bottom.

The forward support bracket is fairly close to where the curved portion of the shield meets the turret side. A small rim runs from this support bracket to the back of the shield, but does not extend to the front of the shield.

The open rear end of the shield allows the machine gun to fold behind this armor protection.

A spotlight is mounted on the turret roof just in front of the hatches. Normally when not in use it was fixed in the down position to protect the lens. (Bob Steinbrunn)

The light's position can be changed by loosening the wing nut on the side of the housing. A cable on a reel inside the turret allows crewmen to move a distance from the tank with the light, which gets its power from the tank battery. (Bill Klingbeil)

The spotlight, seen here in the upright position, swivels and can be detached for ground use. It was powered through a cable from the tank's battery. (Bill Klingbeil)

When the light was stored, a cap is placed over the mount to keep out dirt and moisture. The cap is attached to a chain so that it does not fall off the tank. American tanks were outfitted with numerous practical devices to keep parts from getting lost or misplaced.

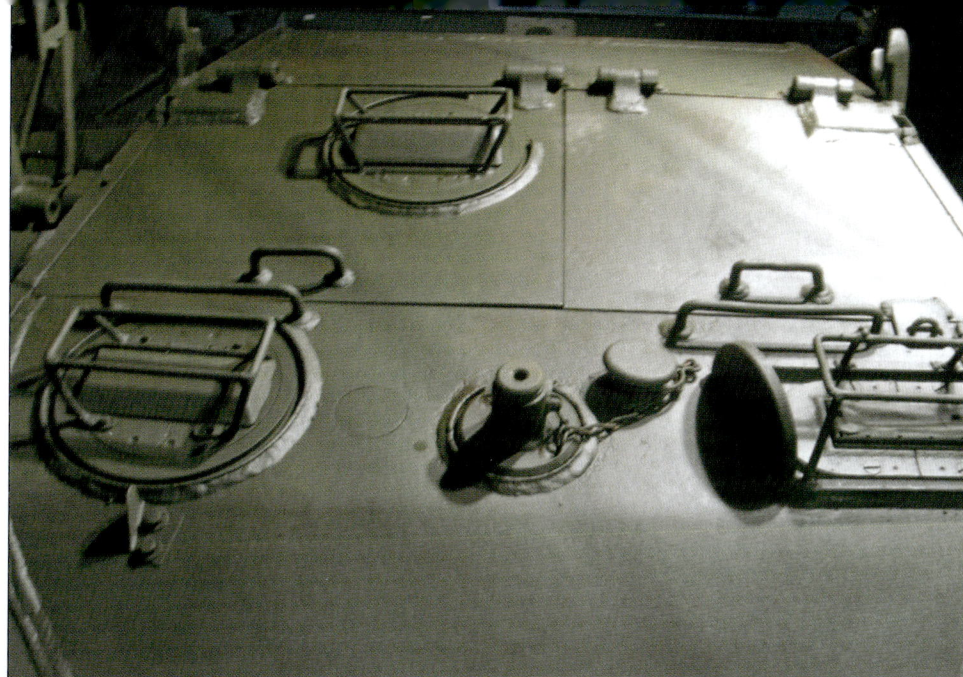

A wire guard protects each periscope from damage. The commander has two periscopes in the hull roof and hatch. The gunner has a single periscope plus a direct sight.

Looking forward, the external lift rings on the hatches are just behind larger handles used by the commander and gunner to steady themselves. When traversing rough ground at its high rate of speed, the M5 could throw the men around and, if not braced, they could suffer injury from the sharp edges of the turret and hatches. (Bill Klingbeil)

The gunner's periscope has side protection since it is the main indirect sight used to locate targets. It does not rotate and its guard is shaped slightly differently from those on the commander's periscopes.

The commander's periscope guards have a more angular shape than the guard on the gunner's periscope. The commander's periscope guards could take a fair amount of abuse but they were commonly seen bent out of shape.

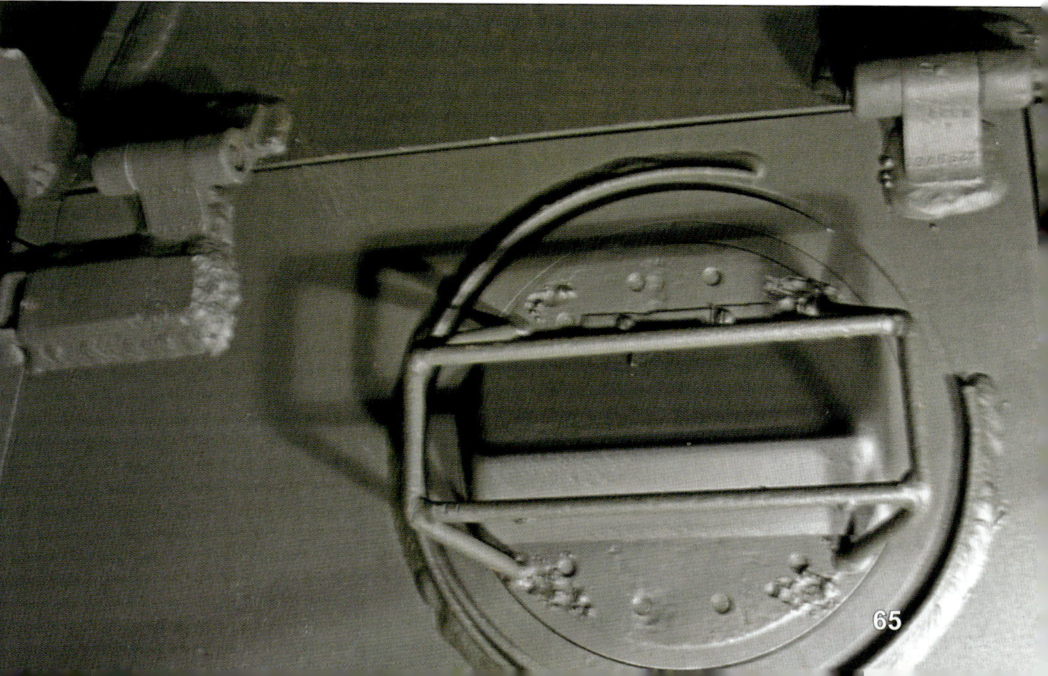

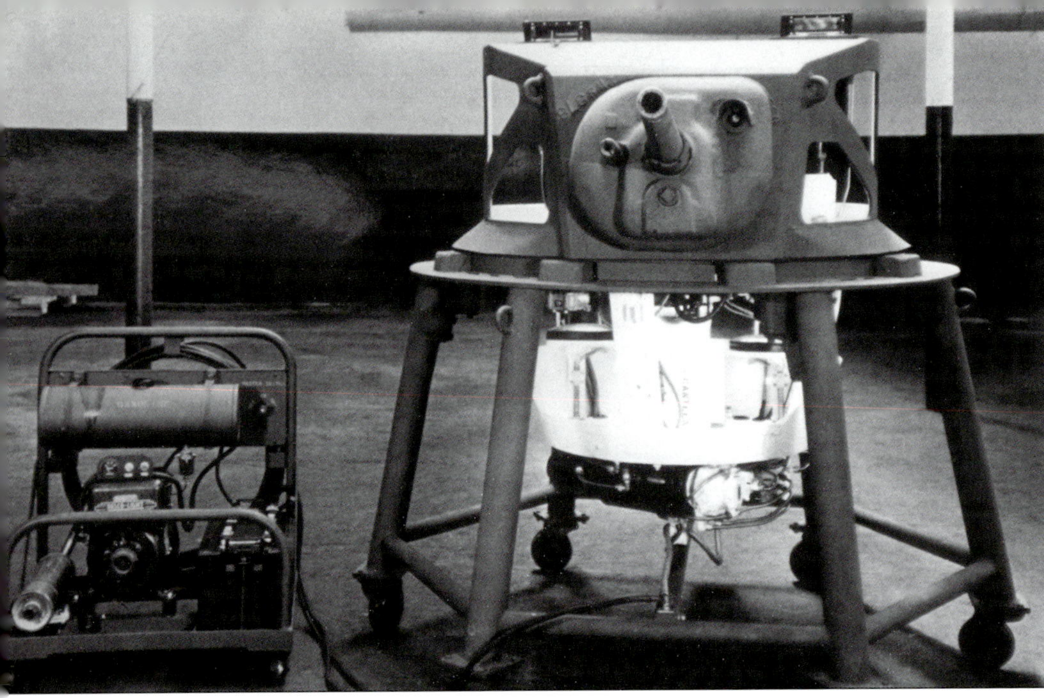

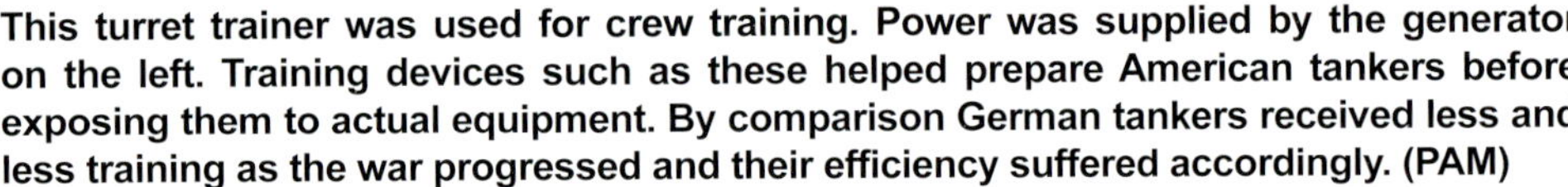
This turret trainer was used for crew training. Power was supplied by the generator on the left. Training devices such as these helped prepare American tankers before exposing them to actual equipment. By comparison German tankers received less and less training as the war progressed and their efficiency suffered accordingly. (PAM)

In this overhead view of the gunner's position, the M4 periscope is on the left and the gun sight is just below the lip of the turret. The bar to the right is a support for the turret hatch when closed. The driver's seat is just visible to the lower left. (Duane Ward)

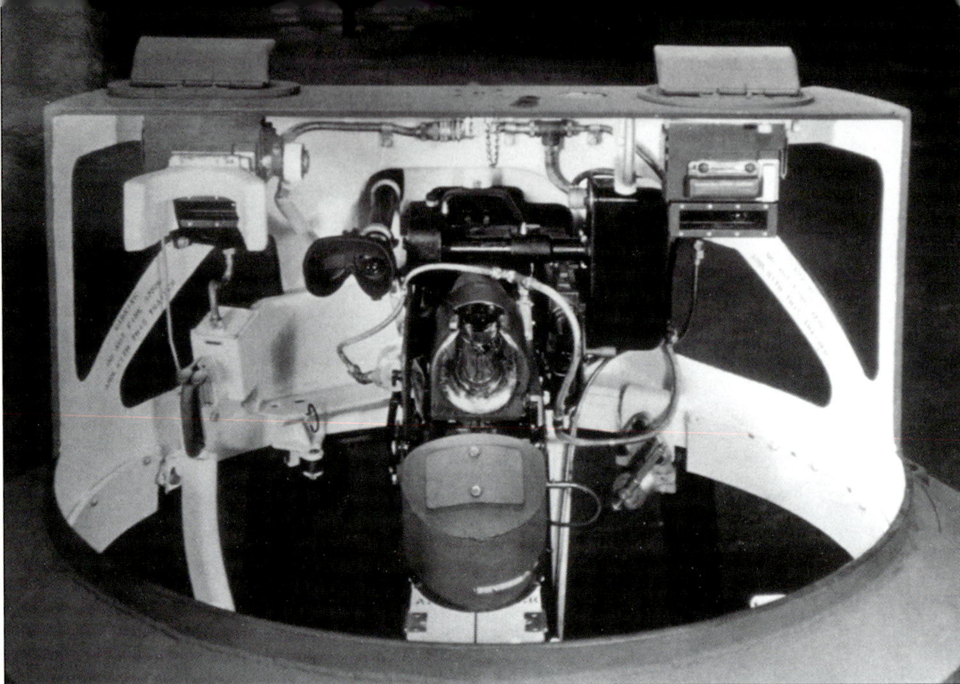

The cut away rear allows instructors to help the crew with all aspects of sighting and firing the 37mm cannon. The M4 and M6 periscopes for the gunner and commander are on the left and right respectively. The gunner's sight is between his periscope and the main gun. (PAM)

The commander's position and M6 periscope pad are below the top of the hatch. The 37mm cannon's breech is on the left. The assistant driver's seat is below. (Duane Ward)

The extended bustle of the M5A1 allows the radio to be mounted in the turret, in contrast to the M5, in which the radio was mounted in the hull. The bustle radio mounting bracket is seen here through the hatch from above.

This rectangular bracket bolted onto the bottom of the turret bustle is designed to hold the radio. The hatch at the back is for the removal of the 37mm cannon. The wire from the radio ran to the external antenna through the hole in the hatch.

On the right side of the turret wall next to the radio is a box to hold .45 caliber ammunition clips for a Thompson sub-machinegun. The latch to the right held the door to the box closed when in place.

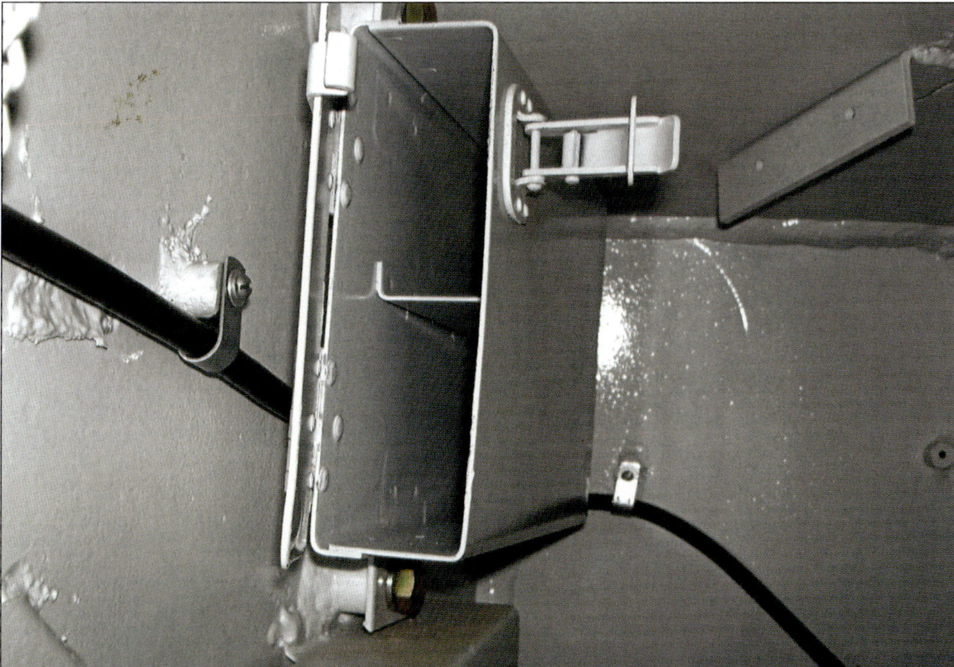

Prongs for holding maps are on the left side of the turret wall next to the radio. The maps were lightly held in place by pressure from the two prongs. After a few weeks in the field the bright white color of the tank interior normally took on a very dingy appearance.

With the canvas cover removed, the radio at the back of the bustle is visible. The M5A1 can carry the SCR 508, 528, or 538. Underneath the radio is the manual rotating mechanism for the turret. (Duane Ward)

Controls and plugs for the radio are seen here in detail. Good communications equipment was a trademark of American vehicles.

The radio is seen here from underneath, mounted in the turret bustle. Various radio combinations allowed effective coordination of movement and support fire between forward elements and rear areas.

The two units of the radio on the right are receivers. The smaller unit to their left is the transmitter. (Duane Ward)

A heavy pad protrudes from the commander's periscope to protect his head from bumps when the tank moves over rough terrain. To the left is the housing for the gun stabilizer system.

The periscope housing is seen here without the periscope and protective head pad. The circular device to the right houses the reel for the cable to the searchlight on the turret top. The cable reel allows the searchlight to be detached from the deck.

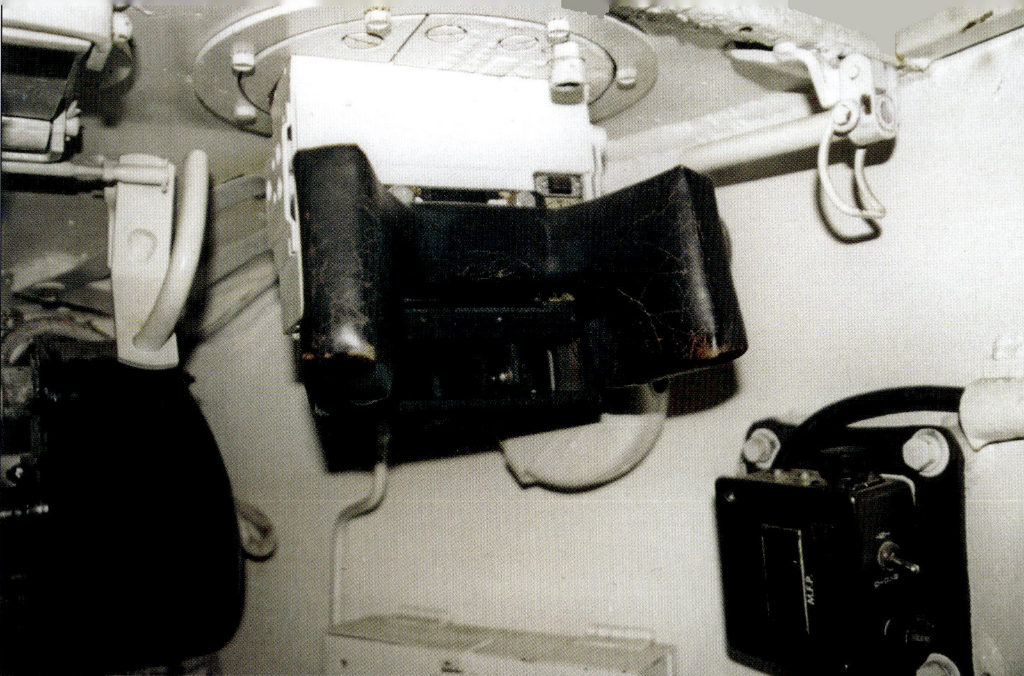

The commander's M6 periscope, which can rotate 360°, is located in the roof. In the bottom corner is the interphone control box. The long pole that ends in a wire hook is designed to secure the hatch. (Duane Ward)

The interphone control box allows connection to either the intercom or radio. The knobs control volume while the switch allows the commander to select which system he wants to use.

The rectangular back box is the gyro control for the hydraulic stabilizer system. The rod to its left is part of the gear system. (Duane Ward)

In addition to a periscope, the gunner had the use of a direct-vision telescopic M70D sight, shown here with its padded eye protector. Visible at upper left is the gunner's M4 periscope. (Duane Ward)

The gunner's station is to the left of the main gun, (not mounted here). Shown here are the gunner's intercom box on the turret roof, a turret light in the upper right, the gun stabilizer panel to the middle left, the periscope holder (barely visible at the extreme left), and the gunner's fire control in the lower left. (Bill Klingbeil)

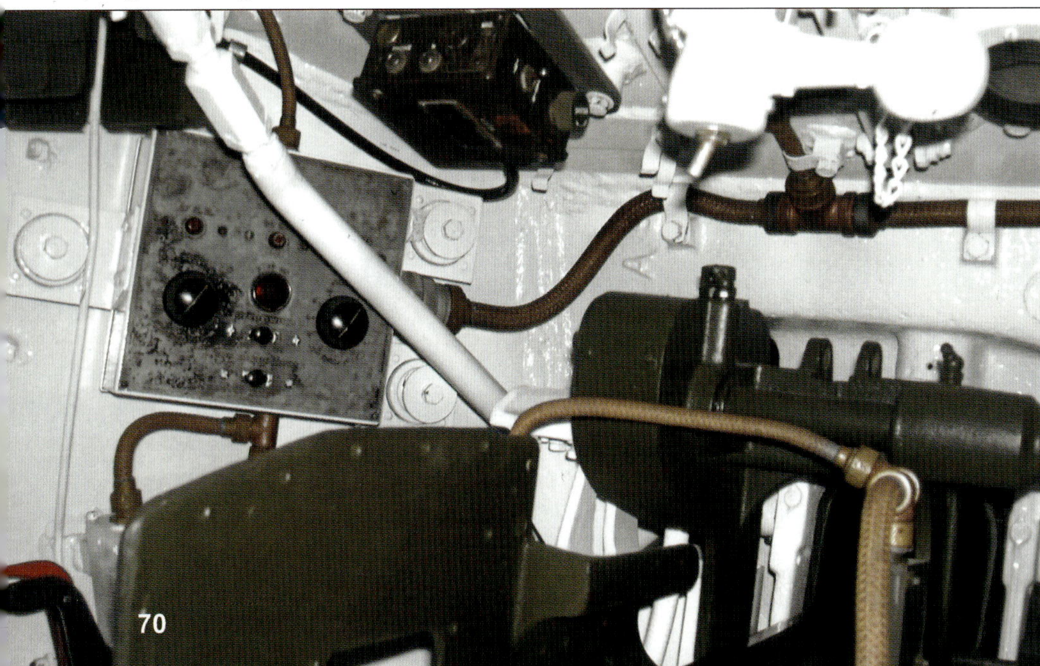

The gun mount and the gyro stabilizer control box are seen here from underneath. The gun stabilizer system helped the M5 to shoot with some accuracy while on the move. Modern systems are, needless to say, more efficient.

The gunner's fire control handle has two triggers, one for the 37m cannon, and the other for the coaxially-mounted .30 caliber machine gun.

The gunner's control is directly under the gun stabilizer system that is mounted on the left side of the turret wall.

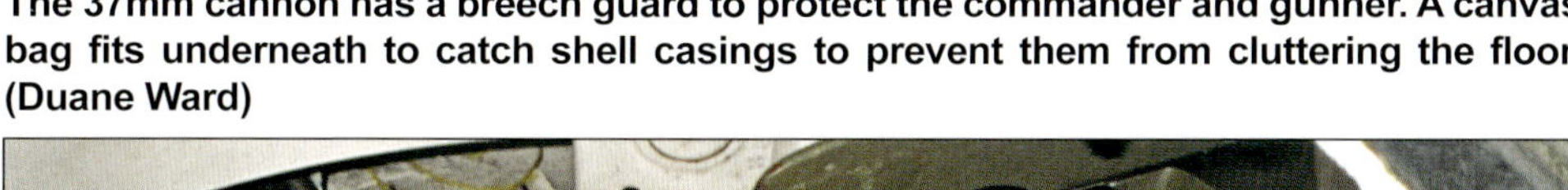

The 37mm cannon has a breech guard to protect the commander and gunner. A canvas bag fits underneath to catch shell casings to prevent them from cluttering the floor. (Duane Ward)

The seats of the commander and gunner are separated by the 37mm breech and breech guard assembly. On the elevator wheel at bottom left is a firing button. The curved plate at the rear deflects shell casings into a canvas bag. (Duane Ward)

The breech guard is in the raised position with the shell casing bag pulled up over it. The bag catches empty shell casings to prevent them from cluttering the turret and possibly jamming the turret basket. (Duane Ward)

To the left of the breech mechanism is the recoil guard. When World War II began in Europe, the 37mm cannon was deemed an adequate anti-tank weapon. By the time U.S. entered the conflict, however, the 37mm had proved wholly inadequate. (Duane Ward)

To the right of the gun mount assembly (seen here without the breech mechanism) is the gyro control box. The combination gun mount is designated M44.

The handle protruding down from the roof is attached to the spotlight and allows the commander to turn the light in the direction he wants. The light switch can be seen on the bottom. The black and green circular objects are interior lights for the crew. (Bill Klingbeil)

The front of the turret basket is tapered. Looking back from the assistant driver's compartment, the bottom of the commander's seat can barely be seen at the top of the spring assembly, above and behind the canteen in the foreground. (Bob Steinbrunn)

The turret basket is circular in shape and has a metal rim that tapers up and outward from the base. (Bill Klingbeil)

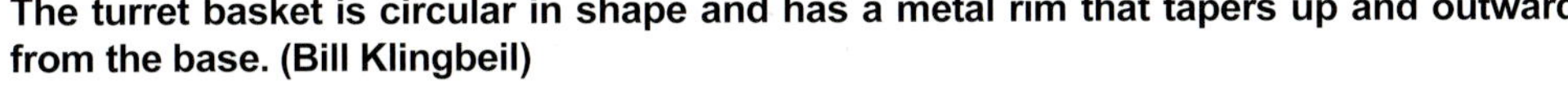

The manual turret traverse mechanism is in the top left of this view from the driver's seat. The box on the pole in the foreground is the roller mechanism mount and support. (Bob Steinbrunn)

The turret basket support doubles as the mount for the commander's and gunner's seats, which can be adjusted up or down. (Bill Klingbeil)

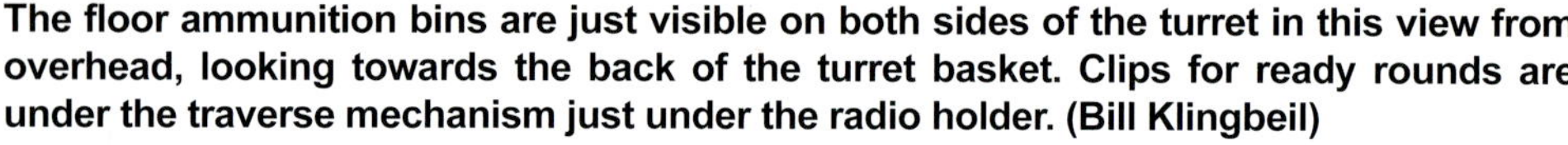

The floor ammunition bins are just visible on both sides of the turret in this view from overhead, looking towards the back of the turret basket. Clips for ready rounds are under the traverse mechanism just under the radio holder. (Bill Klingbeil)

Clips for ready rounds are located on the side of the turret basket. Shells clip into the brackets for easy access during combat. There is also a ready ammunition box located on the turret floor. (Bill Klingbeil)

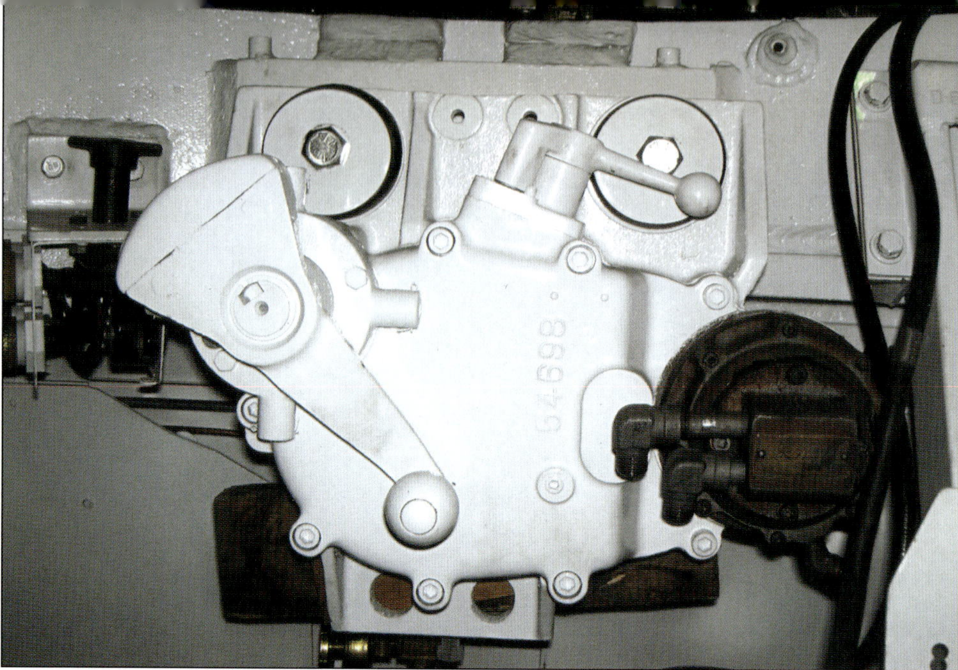

The manual turret traverse mechanism at the back of the turret ring allows the crew to rotate the turret in case the power-traverse unit fails. (Bill Klingbeil)

This overhead view of the manual turret traverse mechanism highlights the fact that U.S. tanks built in redundancy to provide for a variety of options in case of battle damage. Simple construction and interchangeable parts gave U.S. tankers an advantage when it came to maintaining a high availability rate compared to German tanks.

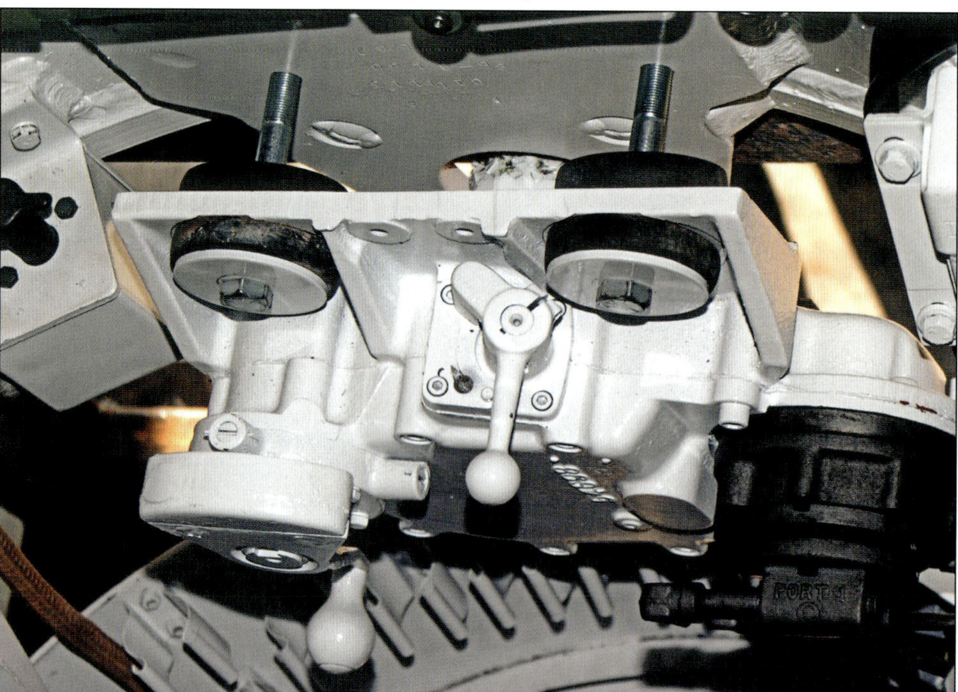

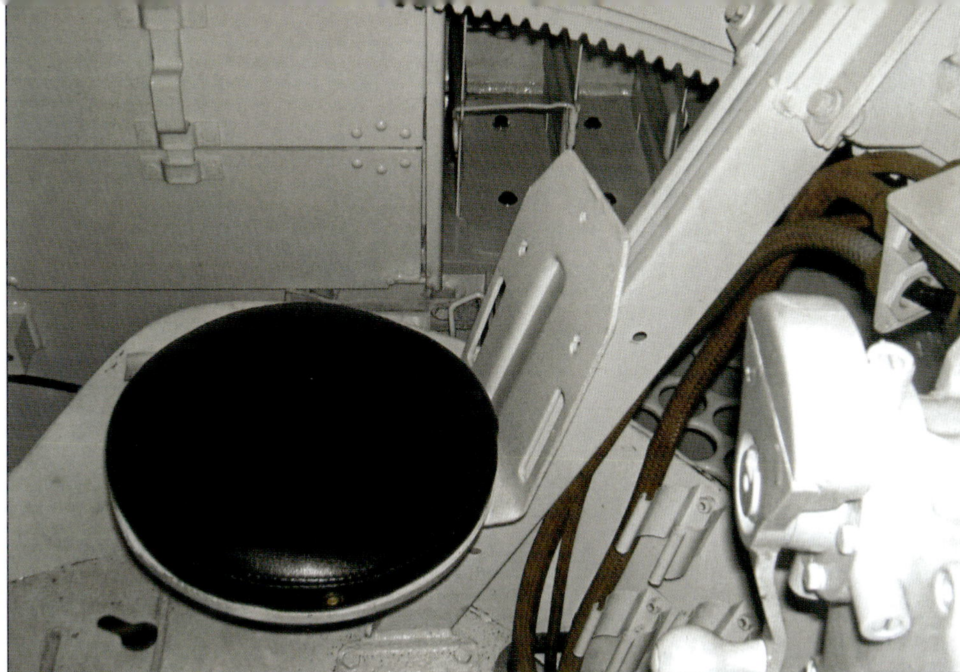

The commander and gunner each had his own seat that could be adjusted as low as the turret floor or as high as the turret ring. The seat is seen here without the back support. (Bill Klingbeil)

Beneath the turret basket is the motor that rotates the turret. In case of a power failure, the crew could rotate the turret by hand.

Identical spring systems facilitate height adjustment on the seats of the commander and gunner. By using a lever, they could move their seats up and down the supporting arms that attached the turret basket to the turret ring. (Bill Klingbeil)

M5

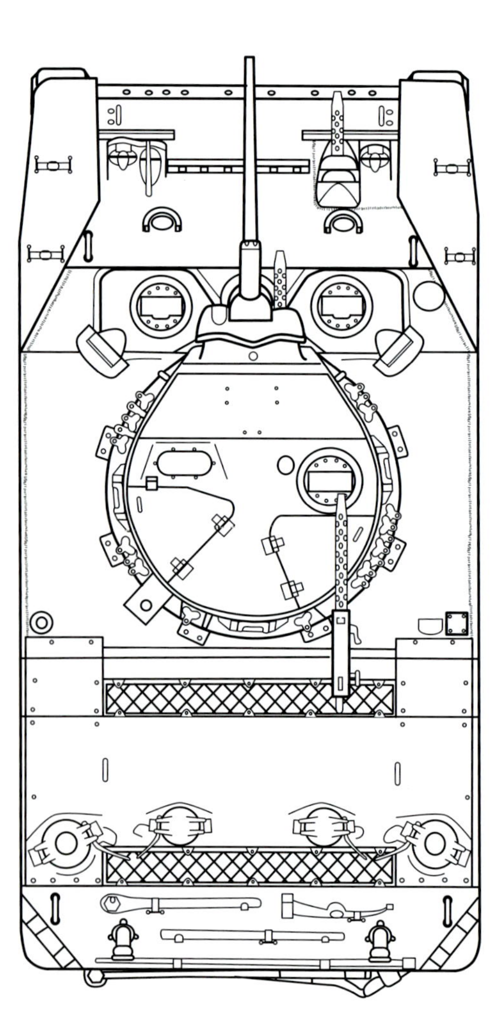

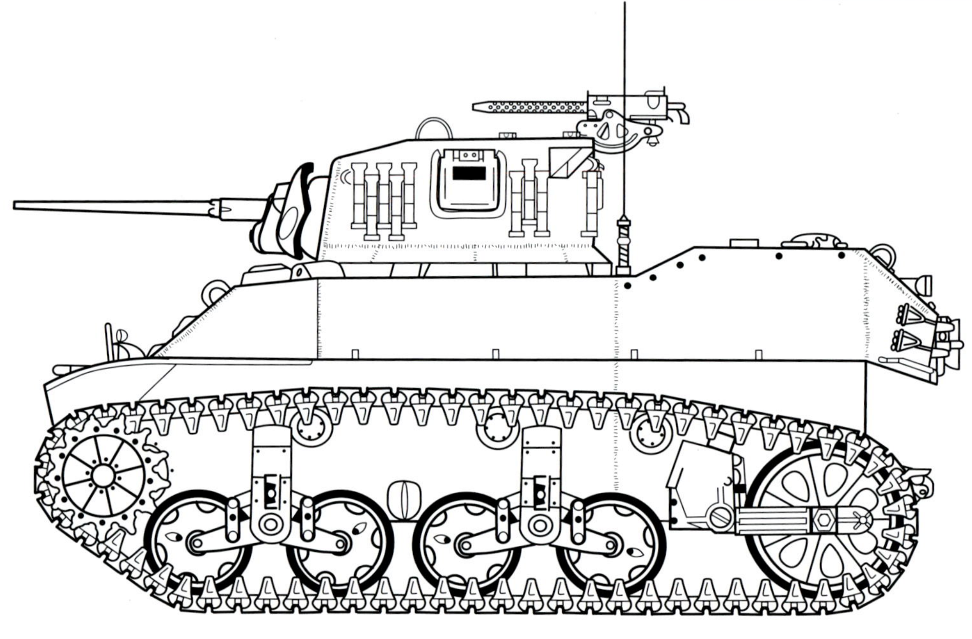

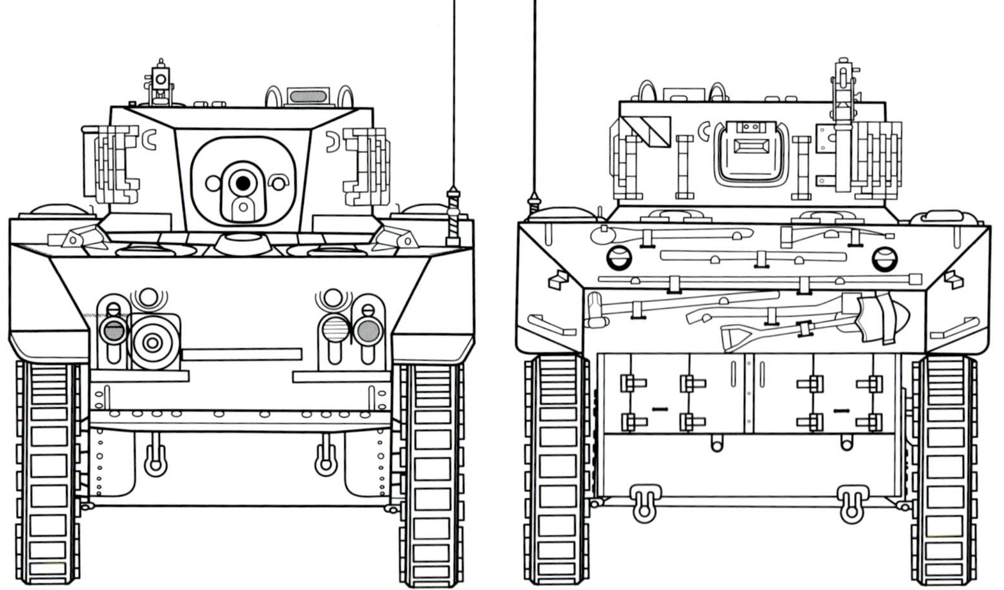

M5A1

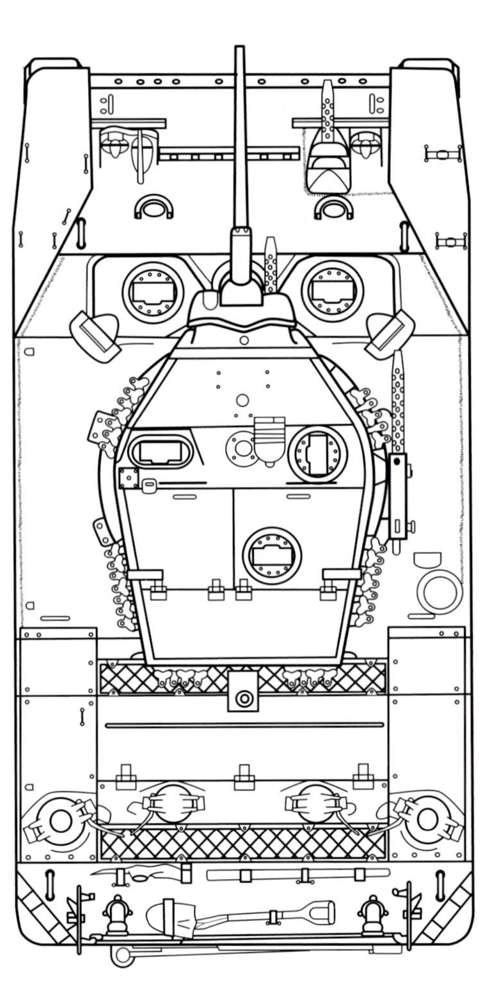

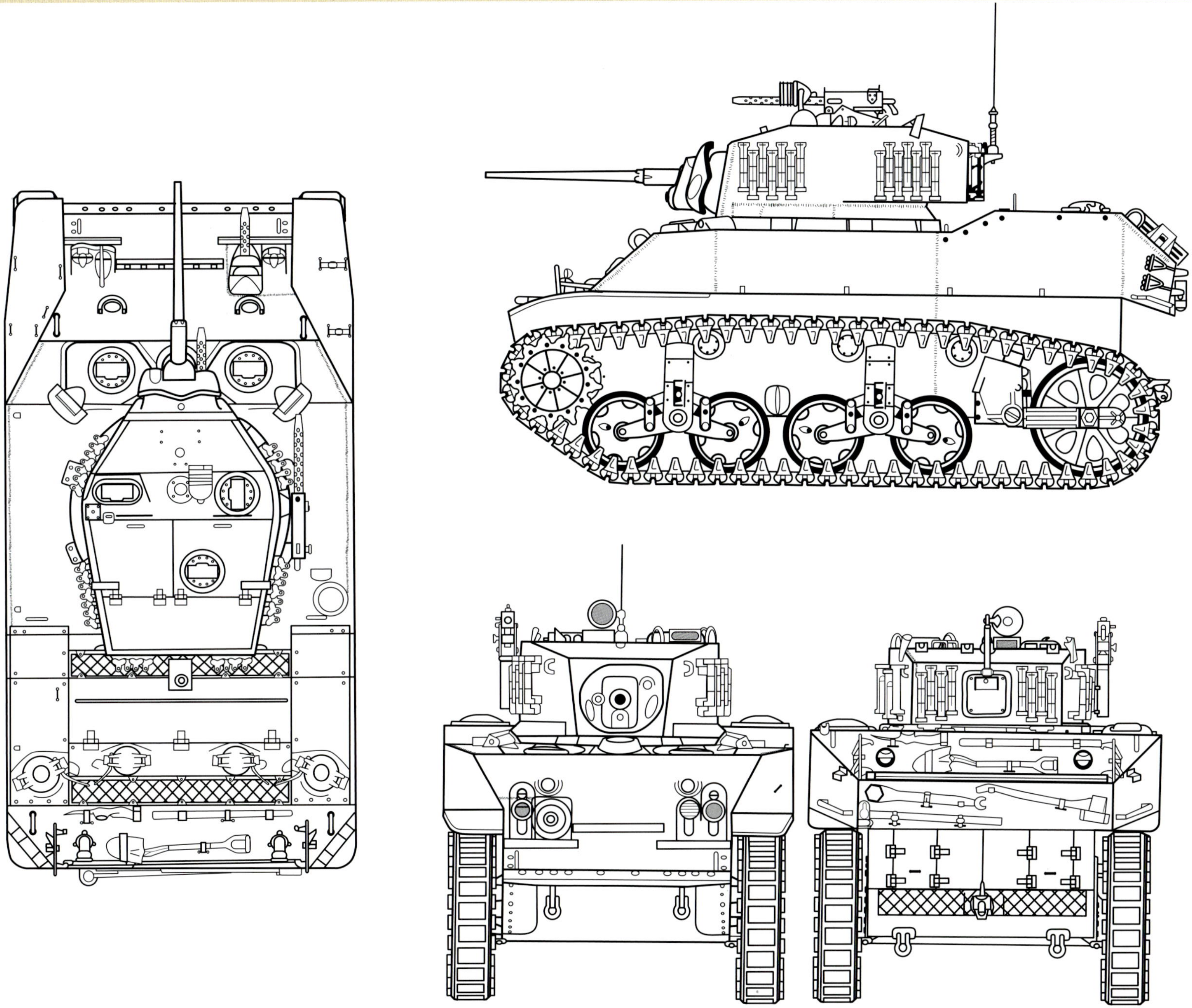

(Left) "L-ON-WHEELS," is an M5A1 of Company "L," 32nd Armored Regiment, 3rd Armored Division, Saint-Fromond, France, in July 1944. The tank is overall olive drab with white registration markings and name. The large "2-3" on the rear of the hull is in yellow. The 3rd Armored Division used such large tactical markings during the summer campaign in 1944, when Allied forces broke out of the Normandy Beachhead and drove across France.

(Right) This M5A1 of an unknown unit, serving in the British Isles during the summer of 1943, is marked with temporary white crosses as a unit of the "Opposing Forces" during war games. The vehicle is overall olive drab with the markings in white. During the invasion buildup, new units were trained in a variety of tactics based on combat experience acquired from action in North Africa and Sicily. Unfortunately there was no training for the extensive Normandy hedgerow terrain.

(Left) An M5A1 is seen in ar-Ribâț ("Rabat"), Morocco, in the summer of 1943, prior to the invasion of Sicily. Over the lusterless Olive Drab base color has been sprayed a camouflage coat of earth yellow. The names on the tank are in white as is the star within the large circle. There is another large star on the top of the turret. The switch back from yellow for the star was a result of the dust covering up the yellow. The white circle was added to help avoid confusion with the German cross.

(Right) "CORSE," an M5A1 of the 1st Squadron, 1st Cuirassiers, 5th French Division, is seen in September 1944. French vehicles were supplied under Lend Lease by the United States and retained their base color of Olive Drab. Depending on the French unit, the additional marking on a vehicle could be quite extensive, as seen here, or relatively limited. French armored units earned a reputation for fierce fighting qualities despite their being supplied with what was frequently regarded as "second hand" equipment.

(Left) "CONCRETE," from Company "C," 33rd Armored Regiment, 3rd Armored Division, served near Saint-Paul-du-Vernay, France, during the summer of 1944. As was typical for this time period the vehicle carries the large tactical markings "C 12" in yellow on its hull side. The "C" represents Company C while the 12 represents the vehicle's number in the company. The tank is overall Olive Drab with white markings. The name of the tank was based on the company's letter.

(Right) An M5A1 of the 11th Armored Division, is pictured near Frankfurt am Main, Germany, in March 1945. This late-production vehicle is in overall Olive Drab with a white star on the turret side. For additional protection against German "Panzerfausts," two large wooden beams have been wired to the side of the hull. Chicken wire has been attached to the turret to hold tree branches for additional camouflage and the crew has piled extra gear and personal items on the rear deck and stowage bin.

(Right) An M5A1 of the 4th Tank Battalion, US Marine Corps, on Kwajalein Atoll, Marshall Islands, February, 1944. It carries a three-tone camouflage scheme of Olive Drab, Sand Yellow, and Red Brown. The name "HUNTER" is inscribed in white on the side of the hull. The Marines used the M3 and M5 extensively early the Pacific War but found its 37m gun inadequate to handle Japanese bunkers. As as result in the latter stages of the war, the M4 became the tank of preference.

(Left) An M5A1 of the 1er Régiment Étranger de Cavalerie, French Foreign Legion, in Indochina, 1946. The overall color is Olive Drab as the French made extensive use of equipment supplied to them under Lend Lease during World War II in the course of their campaign in Indochina from 1945 until 1954. The Foreign Legion used a variety of markings during the campaign and were among the more colorfully marked to see service during the war.

(Right) An M5 of the 70th Tank Battalion is seen during "Operation Torch" in North Africa in November 1942. Many of the M5s used during "Operation Torch" carried prominent American flags on their sides along with large yellow stars on the hull front and sides. It was hoped that the French would not fire on them if they recognized them as Americans. The tank is overall Olive Drab and the registration numbers are in Blue Drab.